Counterintelligence in a Cyber World

Paul A. Watters

Counterintelligence in a Cyber World

 Springer

Paul A. Watters
Cyberstronomy Pty Ltd
Melbourne, VIC, Australia

ISBN 978-3-031-35289-8   ISBN 978-3-031-35287-4   (eBook)
https://doi.org/10.1007/978-3-031-35287-4

This Springer imprint is published by the registered company Springer Nature Switzerland AG
The registered company address is: Gewerbestrasse 11, 6330 Cham, Switzerland

This book is dedicated to my friends and colleagues at Ionize (www.ionize.com.au), Australia's leading sovereign capability, full-spectrum cybersecurity company.

Preface

As we move further into the twenty-first century – what I call the "cyber age" – the field of counterintelligence faces a rapidly evolving landscape of challenges, particularly in the realm of cybersecurity. The threats we face are multifaceted and complex, from state-sponsored cyberattacks to non-state actors seeking to exploit vulnerabilities for personal gain. The lines between traditional espionage and cyber espionage have become increasingly blurred, and the potential consequences of a successful attack are higher than ever before.

To address these challenges, we need to embrace a holistic approach to counterintelligence, one that incorporates traditional techniques alongside cutting-edge technologies and innovative strategies. We must also work to build partnerships and coalitions, both domestically and internationally, in order to share information and resources and to ensure that we are all working toward the same goals.

At the same time, we must remain mindful of the ethical and legal considerations that come with conducting counterintelligence operations. We must ensure that our actions are consistent with our values and with the principles of democracy and free enterprise, and that we do not compromise the privacy and civil liberties of those we seek to protect. This is especially true as the focus of cyber operations extends from the military to the business realm, as businesses begin to adopt (and adapt) classic counterintelligence techniques for the cyber age.

The challenges we face are great, but so too are the opportunities. With the right approach and the right tools, we can meet these challenges head-on and ensure a safer and more secure future for all.

Melbourne, VIC, Australia   Paul A. Watters
March 2023

About the Author

Professor Watters is a trusted cybersecurity advisor and thought leader based in Melbourne, Australia.

Professor Watters is Academic Dean at Academies Australasia Polytechnic, an ASX-listed education provider (ASX:AKG), Strategic Cyber Consultant at Ionize, CEO at Cyberstronomy, and inventor of the 100 Point Cyber Check.

Professor Watters is also Honorary Professor at Macquarie University and Adjunct Professor at La Trobe University. He is a Chartered IT Professional, a Fellow of the British Computer Society, a Senior Member of the IEEE, Member of the ACM, and a Member of the Australian Psychological Society. Professor Watters is a graduate of the University of Cambridge, and an active member of the Senate of the University.

Professor Watters works in three main areas:

- Providing advice on cybersecurity strategy, governance, risk and compliance, and cyber intelligence
- Researching strategies for reducing harm from online child sex abuse, piracy and intellectual property theft, and fraud and scams, phishing, using AI, data mining, and analytics
- Cybersecurity skills assessment and development, including for people on the autism spectrum

For more details, see www.paulwatters.com

Acknowledgments

This book has been planned for several years, but just as I felt I was reaching a conclusion, a new case or technology would get in the way. I would like to acknowledge all those who have contributed to this work, including my colleagues at Ionize, Untapped, Genius Armoury, Academies Australasia Polytechnic, La Trobe University, and Macquarie University.

About the Book

Counterintelligence refers to the efforts undertaken by intelligence agencies to prevent and detect attempts by foreign entities to gather sensitive or classified information from a country's government, military, businesses, or other organizations. In the twenty-first century, counterintelligence has become increasingly important as the world has become more connected through the internet and digital technologies. The rise of cyber espionage and cyberattacks has made it easier for foreign entities to gain access to sensitive information, making it imperative for countries to strengthen their counterintelligence efforts.

Cybersecurity is an essential component of modern counterintelligence efforts. As cyberattacks become more frequent and sophisticated, governments and organizations must implement robust cybersecurity measures to protect their systems and data. However, the fast pace of technological advancements means that cybersecurity is constantly evolving, requiring continuous updates and improvements to stay ahead of emerging threats.

The intersection of counterintelligence and cyber presents unique challenges for governments and organizations. The proliferation of digital technologies has made it easier for foreign entities to engage in cyber espionage and cyberattacks, highlighting the need for effective counterintelligence measures. At the same time, protecting against cyber threats requires a deep understanding of the technologies involved, as well as a willingness to adapt and evolve as the threat landscape changes.

The goal of this book is to provide a detailed sketch for practitioners to deep dive into the topics and concerns that may impact their work, and to consider how broader ethical and legal obligations may inform (or sometimes limit) their professional activities. It also suggests classic techniques and strategies that have worked well in the government sector which can also be readily applied to cyber problems in the commercial sector.

Contents

Abbreviations

GEOINT	Geospatial Intelligence
HUMINT	Human Source Intelligence
IMINT	Imagery Intelligence
OSINT	Open Source Intelligence
SIGINT	Signals Intelligence

Chapter 1
Counterintelligence Theory

Counterintelligence refers to actions taken by a government or other organization (including commercial entities) to prevent hostile or foreign intelligence services (or competitors) from successfully *gathering and collecting intelligence* against it. This can include activities such as *surveillance, deception*, and *infiltration* to prevent *espionage* and *sabotage*.

Intelligence gathering has been an aspect of world history for many years, with examples dating back to ancient civilizations such as Egypt and China. In more recent history, intelligence gathering became more formalized and systematic with the creation of specialized agencies and the use of new technologies.

In more recent years, with the rise of Open Source Intelligence (OSINT), and the ascendancy of hacker culture, red teams and specialized cybercrime gangs, the need for an effective counterintelligence function has moved well beyond the standard list of government agencies that readers will be familiar with, such as the CIA, NSA, MI6, ASIO, and so on. The motivator for this book is to explore document what this means for the discipline of counterintelligence, but also – in practical terms – what are the actions that businesses (especially large, or high value entities) can take to protect themselves from a range of cyber threats, using an intelligence-led approach.

While this may seem like common-sense, surprisingly, cybersecurity tends to focus on building defenses, without any regard to the actual threat actors, as informed by an intelligence function. To go one step further, and invest in a counterintelligence function, must therefore seem beyond the pale. However, the cases outlined in this volume will surely demonstrate the benefits of further investment.

Cybersecurity cannot succeed without intelligence, and intelligence lacking a counterintelligence function is severely limited. Cybersecurity is not only about implementing technical measures to protect networks, applications and systems, but also requires intelligence to understand the threat landscape and potential risks. Intelligence enables organizations to stay ahead of cybercriminals and

P. A. Watters, *Counterintelligence in a Cyber World*,
https://doi.org/10.1007/978-3-031-35287-4_1

state-sponsored hackers, who are constantly evolving their tactics and techniques. Without intelligence, cybersecurity measures may not be effective in preventing attacks.

Counterintelligence is a crucial aspect of cybersecurity that involves identifying and neutralizing foreign intelligence services, cybercriminals, and other threat actors seeking to exploit vulnerabilities in the organization's systems and networks. Intelligence gathering helps organizations to detect and mitigate potential attacks, identify threat actors, and protect sensitive information.

In the twenty-first century, the use of technology and the internet has increased exponentially, leading to an increase in cyber threats. Cybersecurity and counterintelligence are now more important than ever, as cybercriminals and state-sponsored hackers use sophisticated tactics and techniques to breach systems and steal sensitive information. As such, organizations must invest in cybersecurity intelligence capabilities to stay ahead of the curve and protect their critical assets from cyber threats.

Gathering and Collecting Intelligence

Intelligence and Espionage are closely related concepts, but they have some key differences. In the cyber age, perhaps they are merging in the context of "surveillance capitalism" that has been described at length by a number of critics.[1]

Classically, Intelligence refers to the practice of gathering, analyzing, and reporting information for the purpose of informing decisions and actions. It represents a wide-ranging term that encompasses many different undertakings, such as reconnaissance, surveillance, and analysis. Intelligence can be utilized for many purposes, including military operations, policing, and business strategy.

Espionage, alternatively, especially refers to the act of getting classified or confidential material without the owner's knowledge or permission. Espionage is typically associated with governments and military organizations, and it is often used to gain an advantage in a conflict or to protect national security. Espionage can be undertaken by both state and other actors and can incorporate a broad set of activities such as recruiting spies, stealing secrets and technologies, and cyber espionage.

In short, Intelligence is a broader term that encompasses the gathering and analysis of information for various purposes, whereas Espionage is a specific type of intelligence activity that focuses on obtaining secret or confidential information through illegal or unauthorized means.

The focus on this book is really Counterintelligence, as a sub-field on Intelligence; yet, with the merging of interests, operations and strategies in the cyber age by nation states – who may sponsor or permit to operate a range of nefarious activities

---

[1] Read it, and weep: Zuboff, S. (2015). Big other: surveillance capitalism and the prospects of an information civilization. *Journal of information technology, 30*(1), 75–89.

offshore – the distinction may be largely academic in the cyber age. The lessons from historical cases at the nation-state level are just as applicable to corporations seeking to develop a counterintelligence capability.

The History of Counterintelligence

How did we get here, and crucially, where are we going? During the two world wars, intelligence gathering played a critical role in the outcomes. Countries such as the United States and the United Kingdom established dedicated intelligence agencies such as the Office of Strategic Services (OSS) and the British Secret Intelligence Service (SIS) to gather and analyze information.

In the Cold War era, the focus of intelligence shifted towards the gathering of information about foreign governments and militaries, as well as the detection and prevention of espionage. The Central Intelligence Agency (CIA) was created in the United States in 1947, and intelligence agencies of other countries also expanded.

In recent years, the new technology development such as social media, telecommunications and the web has led to an explosion of data and a corresponding increase in the importance of intelligence gathering and analysis by companies and governments. Intelligence agencies and big businesses now use sophisticated algorithms and artificial intelligence to sift through vast amounts of data, and the use of UAVs and drones has greatly expanded their capacity to gather information in difficult to reach areas.

Notably, the use of intelligence may not be limited to governments, as many organizations use intelligence gathering and analysis to protect their interests, whether it is a business trying to protect their trade secrets or a non-profit trying to protect their reputation. Cybercrime gangs and organized crime also invest heavily in Intelligence and other operational activities.

Some sophisticated cybercriminal groups, such as nation-state-sponsored hackers or advanced persistent threat (APT) groups, may engage in counterintelligence activities to protect their own operations from detection and disruption by law enforcement agencies, intelligence services, or rival nation-state actors.

The main characteristics of APTs include:

- *Advanced techniques*: APTs typically use complex methods such as zero-day exploits, malware and social engineering to illegally access a target system or network.
- *Long-term planning*: APTs are designed to be a long-term attack that is often premeditated and accomplished over a period of many weeks or longer. The hackers often study their target's behavior, network architecture, and security measures to plan their attack.
- *Targeted attacks*: APTs are usually targeted at a specific organization, industry, or government agency. The attackers may be after sensitive data such as trade secrets, intellectual property, or personally identifiable information. No more "spray and pray"!

- *Stealthiness*: APTs are designed to be stealthy, meaning they try to remain unde-tected by security systems and avoid triggering alerts. They may use techniques such as encryption and hiding in legitimate network traffic to evade detection.
- *Persistence*: APTs are persistent, meaning that they are designed to maintain a foothold in a target system or network for as long as possible. This allows the attackers to continue to gather information, exfiltrate data, and conduct further attacks over an extended period.
- *Multiple stages*: APTs typically involve multiple stages, with each stage building on the previous one. This allows the attackers to gradually gain more access and control over the target system or network. MITRE ATT&CK provides a mapping and pathway descriptions for how these attacks typically unfold.[2]

These groups may use a range of tactics, such as deploying malware to monitor and control infected systems, using encryption and obfuscation techniques to evade detection, conducting reconnaissance to gather intelligence on potential targets or adversaries, and using social engineering to manipulate individuals or organizations to gain access to sensitive information. Additionally, some cybercrime gangs may collaborate with other criminal groups or nation-state actors to share intelligence or to leverage their capabilities for specific objectives.

Surveillance

Surveillance refers to the collection of information about individuals or groups by government or other organizations. Intelligence services often use surveillance to gather information and protect national security.

Historically, surveillance has been conducted through methods such as wiretapping,[3] mail intercepts, and physical surveillance. With the advent of new technologies, surveillance has become more sophisticated and far-reaching. Intelligence services now use a wide range of tools, including internet monitoring, satellite imagery, and facial recognition software to gather information. It is a topic of more than passing interest to democratic leaders – achieving a balance between overwhelming state and private sector surveillance, and the ever-present and grow-ing cyber threat landscape – is a delicate balance. China's social credit system is one example of where the State has greatly increased its social control to achieve broader national benefits. It is not clear that this level of surveillance would be welcomed by, or accepted by, citizens of liberal democracies. Yet these very same countries engaged in large-scale restrictions of freedom during the COVID era – lockdowns,

---

[2] For details, see https://attack.mitre.org/

[3] For a modern take on wiretapping, see Azab, A., Layton, R., Alazab, M., & Watters, P. (2013, November). Skype traffic classification using cost sensitive algorithms. In *2013 Fourth Cybercrime and Trustworthy Computing Workshop* (pp. 14–21). IEEE.

arbitrary arrests, and so on – all served to illustrate the lust for social control that governments of all stripes and persuasions ultimately yearn for.

In the United States, policing and intelligence agencies such as the Federal Bureau of Investigation (FBI) and the National Security Agency (NSA) conduct surveillance under the authority of laws such as the Foreign Intelligence Surveillance Act (FISA) of 1978.[4] Surveillance is a highly controversial topic, yet central to the effectiveness of counterintelligence. After all, there can be no "spies" without any "spying"!

While internet surveillance has become commonplace, there are several technical limitations of internet surveillance that can impact its effectiveness. Described below are some of the main limitations:

- *Encryption*: Many online services use encryption to protect user data and communications. This can make it difficult for surveillance agencies (or businesses!) to intercept and decipher the data, even if they can access it.[5]
- *Anonymity*: It's possible to utilize applications such as virtual private networks (VPNs) or the Tor network to mask the origin of activity, making it difficult to trace back to the user.[6]
- *Data volume*: The sheer volume of internet traffic can make it difficult to monitor all activity. Surveillance agencies need to prioritize what data they collect and analyze, and businesses must determine the localized scope of their own collections and operations.
- *Data retention*: Many online services only retain data for a limited period, making it difficult to access historical data that may be relevant to an investigation.[7]
- *False positives*: Automated surveillance systems can generate false positives, which can waste resources and cause privacy concerns if innocent users are targeted. Try and avoid!
- *Legal limitations*: Internet surveillance is subject to legal limitations, such as the requirement for warrants or restrictions on what categories of data can be collected.

The use of surveillance by intelligence services has also been the subject of controversy, with concerns raised about privacy and civil liberties. Some critics argue that the increased use of surveillance represents a violation of individual rights, while

---

[4] For details, see https://bja.ojp.gov/program/it/privacy-civil-liberties/authorities/statutes/1286

[5] Difficult, but its presence may still inform an appropriate response, see Ceesay, E. N., Do, T. N., & Watters, P. A. (2017, July). Cyber-Situational Awareness in the Presence of Encryption. In *2017 IEEE 7th Annual International Conference on CYBER Technology in Automation, Control, and Intelligent Systems (CYBER)* (pp. 1621–1626). IEEE.

[6] Ironically, sponsored by the United States government, for an outline, see Dingledine, R., Mathewson, N., & Syverson, P. (2004). *Tor: The second-generation onion router*. Naval Research Lab Washington DC.

[7] In some countries like Australia, there is a statutory data retention period, for details, see https://www.homeaffairs.gov.au/about-us/our-portfolios/national-security/lawful-access-telecommunications/data-retention-obligations

others argue that it is necessary to protect national security. These are non-trivial and important questions.

Recently, surveillance methods and the collection of personal data have been the subject of much debate, with many Governments, intelligence agencies and private companies have been accused of using it excessively or without proper oversight and without protecting the privacy of citizens.

Deception

Deception refers to the use of false information or tactics to mislead or manipulate an individual or group by government or other organizations. Intelligence services often use deception to protect national security and gain an advantage over adversaries.

Deception can take many forms, including the use of false flags, disinformation, and impersonation.[8] False flags refer to the use of disguises or cover stories to conceal the identity or intentions of an individual or group. Disinformation refers to the spread of false information with the intent to deceive. Impersonation refers to the use of false identities or disguises to infiltrate an organization or gain the trust of an individual.

In the realm of intelligence gathering, deception can be used to mislead an opponent or to protect covert operations. For example, a spy agency might use deception to conceal the identity of an agent or to create the impression that they have more resources or capabilities than they actually do.

Deception can also be used in psychological operations or "psyops", which aim to change the decision-making of people or groups.[9] For example, an intelligence service might use psyops to spread rumors or propaganda to disrupt or demoralize an opposing force. In the era of social media, the delivery of propaganda, misinformation and disinformation have had very significant consequences, even to the extent of swinging elections.[10]

As an example, deception played a significant role in the 2016 U.S. presidential election.[11] There were multiple instances of misinformation, disinformation, and propaganda campaigns designed to deceive voters and sway the election in favor of certain candidates. Described below are some examples:

---

[8] For an example, see Watters, P. A. (2013). Modelling the effect of deception on investigations using open source intelligence (OSINT). *Journal of Money Laundering Control*, *16*(3), 238–248.

[9] For an overview, see Narula, S. (2004). Psychological operations (PSYOPs): A conceptual overview. *Strategic Analysis*, *28*(1), 177–192.

[10] A seriously complex arena! For a review, see https://www.theverge.com/2022/9/19/23360688/pentagon-review-military-influence-operations-social-media

[11] For a complete analysis, see McCombie, S., Uhlmann, A. J., & Morrison, S. (2020). The US 2016 presidential election & Russia's troll farms. *Intelligence and National Security*, *35*(1), 95–114.

- *Russian interference*: The U.S. intelligence community concluded that Russia conducted a campaign to interfere in the 2016 election using disinformation and propaganda. The campaign utilized social media to disseminate false information and sow division among U.S. voters.
- *Fake news*: There were numerous instances of fake news stories being disseminated on social media platforms during the election.[12] Some of these stories were designed to be deliberately misleading or false, with the intention of influencing voters' opinions.
- *Hacking*: The hacking of political organizations and individuals' email accounts was used to steal sensitive information and then leak it to the public. This was intended to damage the reputation of certain candidates and influence the outcome of the election.[13]
- *Voter suppression*: There were reports of targeted disinformation campaigns aimed at suppressing the vote in certain areas, particularly among minority communities.[14]

Please note that deception can be a controversial tactic, as it can be seen as a violation of trust and can have negative consequences if discovered. In addition, the use of deception can be difficult to detect and control, and it can backfire if the person or group being deceived is able to see through the deception. Ethical issues with the use of deception are complex and longstanding.

Infiltration

Infiltration refers to the act of placing covert agents or informants within an organization or group to gather information or influence its actions. Intelligence services often use infiltration to get into an organization and disrupt its activities.

The process of infiltration typically begins with the identification of a target organization or group. Intelligence agencies will then gather information about the group's structure, leadership, and activities to identify potential vulnerabilities or weaknesses.

Once a potential target has been identified, the intelligence service will recruit and train individuals to infiltrate the organization. These individuals may be recruited from within the group, or they may be outsiders who are able to gain the trust of the group's members.

---

[12] For a review of algorithmic issues in fake detection, see Watters, P., & Layton, R. (2011, September). Fake file detection in P2P networks by consensus and reputation. In *2011 First International Workshop on Complexity and Data Mining* (pp. 80–83). IEEE.

[13] Oh yes! This was a big one, for details, see https://www.washingtonpost.com/world/national-security/how-the-russians-hacked-the-dnc-and-passed-its-emails-to-wikileaks/2018/07/13/af19a828-86c3-11e8-8553-a3ce89036c78_story.html

[14] Not a hypothetical! It happened - https://www.brennancenter.org/our-work/research-reports/digital-disinformation-and-vote-suppression

The infiltrator will then use their position within the group to gather information or influence its actions. This can include collecting intelligence on the group's plans, activities, and leadership; identifying potential vulnerabilities; and reporting back to the intelligence agency.

Please note that infiltration can be a highly effective tactic, but it also carries significant risks. If the infiltrator is discovered, it can damage the reputation of the intelligence service and put the infiltrator in danger. In addition, infiltration can be a violation of the trust of the group or organization, and it can be difficult to control the actions of the infiltrator once they are inside the target group.

Note that in the cyber age, infiltration can be performed by an effective hacking (red) team; physical proximity is no longer a requirement. Agencies and businesses need to consider how this reshaping of infiltration tactics must also transform strategic thinking, especially in relation to the insider threat.

Insider threats refer to the risks that an individual within an organization, such as an employee or contractor, will use their access to sensitive information or systems for malicious purposes. This can include stealing confidential information, introducing malware or conducting other types of attacks. The focus here is on the actions of an individual who has legitimate access to the systems or information in question, but who chooses to use that access for nefarious purposes.

Infiltration, on the other hand, refers to an external threat where an attacker gains unauthorized access to an organization's systems or information by bypassing security measures. In this scenario, the attacker may use tactics such as social engineering or exploiting vulnerabilities to gain a foothold in the target system. The focus here is on the external threat actor who is attempting to obtain sensitive information or penetrate systems, typically to carry out espionage, theft, or sabotage.

One example of infiltration in the cyber age is the case of Stuxnet, a computer worm that was revealed in 2010 and was intended to penetrate and destroy industrial control systems, specifically those used in Iran's nuclear program.[15]

The virus was initially spread through infected USB drives and targeted Siemens industrial control systems. It was able to exploit zero-day vulnerabilities to spread through networks and eventually reach its target systems. Once there, it would reprogram the industrial controllers to operate in ways that would cause physical damage to the equipment, such as causing centrifuges to spin too fast and causing them to fail.

The attack was sophisticated and well-planned, and it is believed that it was a joint effort between the United States and Israel. Attackers infiltrated the Iranian atomic platform and produce substantial harm to their plant without physical presence or intervention. No "boots on the ground"!

The Stuxnet attack was significant because it demonstrated the potential for cyber-attacks to cause physical damage to critical infrastructure. It also highlighted the importance of securing industrial control systems and the potential

---

[15] For a complete description, see Collins, S., & McCombie, S. (2012). Stuxnet: the emergence of a new cyber weapon and its implications. *Journal of Policing, Intelligence and Counter Terrorism*, 7(1), 80–91.

consequences of a successful attack. The incident has since led to increased awareness and investment in securing critical infrastructure from cyber threats.[16]

Sabotage

Sabotage refers to the act of intentionally causing damage or destruction to equipment, facilities, or infrastructure to disrupt the operations of an organization or government. Intelligence services may use sabotage to weaken an opposing force or to
gain an advantage in a conflict.

Sabotage can take many forms, including destruction of equipment, disruption of
supply lines, and cyber-attacks. Intelligence services may carry out sabotage operations themselves, or they may use agents or proxies to carry out the attacks.

Sabotage can be a highly effective tactic, as it can disrupt the operations of an
opposing force and create confusion and chaos. However, it can also be a controversial tactic, as it can cause harm to civilians and can be seen as violating international
law. In addition, sabotage can be difficult to control and may have unintended
consequences.

It is also important to note that sabotage is utilized at both a state and non-state
level, depending on the group or organization that is conducting it. Some terrorist
groups or criminal organizations may use sabotage to achieve their goals.

A good example of cyber sabotage is a Distributed Denial of Service (DDoS)
attack - thousands of computers are coordinated to transmit vast volumes of mal-
formed packets to block legitimate access to a webserver or other internet-connected
host. The results can be devastating.

There have been several noteworthy DDoS attacks that involved sabotage, targeting organizations for political or ideological reasons. Some of these cases include:

1. *Operation Payback*: In 2010, the group "Anonymous" launched DDoS attacks
   against several organizations, including Visa, Mastercard, and PayPal, after they
   suspended payments to WikiLeaks. The attacks were aimed at disrupting the
   operations of these organizations and sending a message of protest against their
   actions.[17]
2. *Mirai botnet*: In 2016, the Mirai botnet was used to launch DDoS attacks against
   several high-profile websites, including Twitter, Reddit, and Netflix. The botnet
   was comprised of IoT devices that had been compromised by hackers, and the
   attacks were aimed at causing widespread disruption and damaging the reputation of the targeted companies.[18]

---

[16] For an overview, see Goyal, R., Sharma, S., Bevinakoppa, S., & Watters, P. (2012). Obfuscation
of stuxnet and flame malware. *Latest Trends in Applied Informatics and Computing*, *150*, 154.

[17] For a review, see Mansfield-Devine, S. (2011). Anonymous: serious threat or mere annoyance?.
Network Security, *2011*(1), 4–10.

[18] For technical details, see Antonakakis, M., April, T., Bailey, M., Bernhard, M., Bursztein, E.,
Cochran, J., ... & Zhou, Y. (2017). Understanding the mirai botnet. In *26th {USENIX} security
symposium ({USENIX} Security 17)* (pp. 1093–1110).

3. *Operation Ababil*: In 2012 and 2013, a group called the "Cutting Sword of Justice" used DDoS against financial organizations like Bank of America, JPMorgan Chase, and Wells Fargo. The attacks were motivated by anger over an anti-Islam video posted on YouTube and were aimed at disrupting the banks' online services and causing financial damage.[19]

In all these cases, the DDoS attacks were used as a tool for sabotage, either to disrupt the operations of the targeted organizations or to make a political statement. The attacks highlight the potential for cybercriminals and hacktivists to use DDoS as a means of achieving their goals, and the need for organizations to be prepared to defend against such attacks.

Successful Counterintelligence Programs

There are numerous historical examples of successful counterintelligence programs in recent history:

- *The Venona Project*: This was a US counterintelligence effort during the Cold War that aimed to intercept and decrypt Soviet intelligence messages. The project was successful in identifying and revealing the identities of several Soviet spies operating within the US government and military, infamously including the Rosenbergs.[20]
- *Operation Mincemeat*: This was a British counterintelligence operation during World War II that involved planting false information with a corpse to deceive the Germans about the Allies' plans for an invasion of Italy. The operation was successful in convincing the Germans to divert troops away from the actual invasion site, helping to secure a swift victory for the Allies.[21]
- *The Cambridge Five*: This was a group of Soviet spies who infiltrated British intelligence and government agencies during the Cold War. The group included individuals such as Kim Philby, Guy Burgess, and Donald Maclean, who were able to provide valuable information to the Soviet Union for many years before being exposed and arrested.[22]

Please note that these are just a few examples of counterintelligence success, there are many other operations and efforts that have been successful in preventing or undermining espionage and sabotage activities. It is unclear whether classical counterintelligence techniques can be at all effective in the cyber age.

---

[19] For an outline, see Iasiello, E. (2013, June). Cyber attack: A dull tool to shape foreign policy. In *2013 5th International Conference on Cyber Conflict (CYCON 2013)* (pp. 1–18). IEEE.

[20] Read the book: Haynes, J. E., & Klehr, H. (2008). Venona. In *Venona*. Yale University Press.

[21] For a military analysis, see Sellers, B. E. (2009). *Case study: Operation Mincemeat*. AIR COMMAND AND STAFF COLL MAXWELL AFB AL.

[22] For a review, see Friend, J. W. (2000). Uncovering Stalin's Spies. *International Journal of Intelligence and CounterIntelligence, 13*(3), 381–384.

A more recent success in the cyber realm was the FBI's Operation Tovar,[23] which targeted the Gameover Zeus botnet. The operation was a collaboration between law enforcement agencies in over 10 countries, as well as private sector companies. The operation successfully took down the botnet and its associated infrastructure, preventing the loss of millions of dollars in stolen funds.

Another noteworthy success was the disruption of the Lazarus Group,[24] a hacking group believed to be affiliated with the North Korean government. In 2017, the group was responsible for the WannaCry ransomware incident, affecting many hosts globally. A collaborative effort between the United States, United Kingdom, and South Korea tracked down and disrupted the group's infrastructure, limiting their ability to carry out further attacks.

The WannaCry ransomware operates through encrypting files on hosts and then extorting users and to regain access. Once the ransomware infects a system, it spreads rapidly to other vulnerable machines on the same network.[25] This is accomplished through a worm-like behavior that allows the ransomware to self-replicate and spread to other systems without any user interaction.[26]

When WannaCry infects a system, it first checks to see if the EternalBlue vulnerability is present. If it is, the ransomware uses the vulnerability to install itself on the system and execute its malicious code. Once installed, WannaCry uses a combination of symmetric and asymmetric encryption to encrypt data on hosts system, preventing user access.

The ransomware then show a message on the infected system's display requiring payment in trade for access. The extortion demands varied, but typically ranged from several hundred to several thousand dollars in bitcoin.

In addition to these examples, there have been many other successful counterintelligence operations targeting cyber threats, including the disruption of botnets,[27] takedowns of dark web marketplaces, and the arrest and prosecution of cybercriminals. However, as the cyber threat landscape continues to evolve and become more complex, the challenges of conducting effective counterintelligence operations will only increase.

---

[23] For a review, see Hernandez-Castro, J., Cartwright, E., & Stepanova, A. (2017). Economic analysis of ransomware. *arXiv preprint arXiv:1703.06660*.

[24] A highly recommended podcast is available here: https://www.bbc.co.uk/programmes/w13xtvg9/episodes/downloads

[25] For a technical analysis, see McIntosh, T. R., Jang-Jaccard, J., & Watters, P. A. (2018). Large scale behavioral analysis of ransomware attacks. In *Neural Information Processing: 25th International Conference, ICONIP 2018, Siem Reap, Cambodia, December 13–16, 2018, Proceedings, Part VI 25* (pp. 217–229). Springer International Publishing.

[26] For a broad discussion, see McIntosh, T., Kayes, A. S. M., Chen, Y. P. P., Ng, A., & Watters, P. (2023). Applying Staged Event-Driven Access Control to Combat Ransomware. *Computers & Security*, 103160.

[27] For a review of botnets, see Zhang, L., Yu, S., Wu, D., & Watters, P. (2011, November). A survey on latest botnet attack and defense. In *2011 IEEE 10th International Conference on Trust, Security and Privacy in Computing and Communications* (pp. 53–60). IEEE.

The Rise of Cybersecurity

This book is about the cyber context in which counterintelligence now finds itself. It would be a vast understatement to say that cyber has completely changed the traditional techniques of counterintelligence, and the goal of this book is to provide practical guidance – grounded in theory – about how to design and execute a successful counterintelligence program in the cyber age. There are some immediate examples of how cyber has radically shaped counterintelligence:

1. *Increased use of digital surveillance*: With social media especially, intelligence agencies have access to a vast amount of data that can be used for surveillance. This includes data from social media, email, messaging apps, and other online sources. As a result, counterintelligence agencies have been able to observe the online activities of potential spies and other adversaries more effectively.
2. *Cyber espionage*: As technology has advanced, so too can espionage activities be carried out online. This includes hacking into networks and systems to steal sensitive information or using malware and other tools to hack a target's system or other device. Cyber espionage has made it easier for intelligence agencies to access sensitive information and has also increased the risk of data breaches and other cyber-attacks.
3. *The use of encryption*: The increasing use of encryption has made it more difficult for intelligence agencies to monitor and intercept communications. This has forced counterintelligence agencies to create new opportunities to bypass encryption and gain access to sensitive information.
4. *The use of social engineering*: Cyber criminals and intelligence agencies have begun to trick users into revealing data or authentication credentials. This can include phishing or other scams,[28] pretexting, and other tactics that exploit human psychology to gain access to sensitive information.
5. *The use of data mining and related tehnologies*: Intelligence agencies are increasingly using Artificial Intelligence (AI), Machine Learning (ML) and related techniques to analyze large amounts of data and identify patterns or anomalies that may indicate the presence of a spy or other threat. This technology can help counterintelligence agencies detect and track potential adversaries more effectively.

These concepts are further expanded below and are described in finer detail in the later chapters of this book. A further change is that the private sector is now much more engaged in various forms of intelligence gathering; sometimes, there is an interaction with, and cross-over between, corporate and government interests in this respect.[29]

---

[28] For examples, see Layton, R., Watters, P., & Dazeley, R. (2012, October). Unsupervised authorship analysis of phishing webpages. In *2012 International Symposium on Communications and Information Technologies (ISCIT)* (pp. 1104–1109). IEEE.

[29] Australia's Trusted Information Sharing Network (TISN) is one example of this: https://www.cisc.gov.au/engagement/trusted-information-sharing-network

Digital Surveillance

Digital surveillance refers to the practice of using digital technology to monitor, track, and collect information about individuals or groups. This can include monitoring internet activity, tracking the location of mobile devices, and using cameras and other sensors to record activity. Digital surveillance is often used by intelligence and law enforcement agencies to gather information about potential threats, to track the activities of suspected criminals or terrorists, or to monitor the activities of foreign governments or organizations.

There are a variety of tools and techniques used for digital surveillance, including:

- *Data mining*: using software to analyze vast data quantities from a range of sources, like social media, email, and chat logs, to identify patterns or anomalies that may indicate criminal or terrorist activity.[30]
- *Network monitoring*: using software to monitor and analyze the activity on a computer network, such as the internet or a company's internal network, to detect suspicious activity or attempts to access sensitive information.
- *Cell-site simulators* also known as Stingrays, are devices utilized by police agencies to track locations of mobile devices via mimicking a cell tower.
- *Biometric surveillance*: using facial features, fingerprints, or iris scans to identify and track individuals.

Please note that digital surveillance has raised several concerns regarding *privacy*, *civil liberties*, and *human rights*. Some experts argue that digital surveillance could be used to target and monitor individuals based on their race, religion, or political beliefs, and that it could be used to suppress dissent and stifle free speech. These concerns extend to the use of algorithms which may an inbuilt bias which results in unreasonably intrusive surveillance or discrimination which is not at all justified.

Cyber Espionage

This refers to using digital technology to obtain sensitive or confidential information without the permission of the person or organization that holds it. Some of the characteristics of cyber espionage include:

- *Stealth*: Cyber espionage utilizes sophisticated tools and techniques to access a target's network or computer without being detected. This may include the use of malware, social engineering tactics, or other methods to bypass security measures.

---

[30] For a literature survey, see Sarker, I. H., Kayes, A. S. M., Badsha, S., Alqahtani, H., Watters, P., & Ng, A. (2020). Cybersecurity data science: an overview from machine learning perspective. *Journal of Big data*, 7, 1–29.

- *Remote access*: Cyber espionage often allows the attacker to access sensitive information from a remote location, making it difficult to trace the origin of the attack.
- *Targeting specific information*: Cyber espionage campaigns are often focused on stealing specific types of information such as intellectual property, classified documents, trade secrets, and sensitive personal information.
- *Use of advanced tools and techniques*: Cyber espionage often involves the use of advanced tools and techniques such as malware, zero-day exploits, and custom-made malware to access a system.
- *Attribution*: Cyber espionage is hard to attribute to a certain country or non-state actor.[31] Nation-state hackers often use tactics to hide their origin, including using compromised systems as jump-off points for their attacks, using encryption to conceal their communications, and deploying malware that erases its tracks.
- *Persistence*: Cyber espionage campaigns are often long-term in nature, with attackers remaining on a target's network for extended periods of time to gather as much information as possible.
- *Impactful results*: Cyber espionage can result in serious effects like financial losses, harm to reputations, and reduced competitive advantage.

Please note that cyber espionage is considered a criminal activity by many countries and is prohibited under international laws. This theme will be discussed in greater detail in Chap. 11.

The Challenge of Encryption

Encryption involves converting a "plaintext" into a format which is unreadable by anyone except those who possess the key to decrypt it. This allows sensitive information to be transmitted securely and keeps it protected from unauthorized access. Encryption can use a range of different algorithms and encryption keys. The difficulty of cracking encryption can vary depending on the specific encryption algorithm and key length used. Generally, the longer the encryption key, the more secure the encryption. However, even a long key can be cracked if the encryption algorithm has been compromised or if there is a vulnerability in the implementation of the encryption.

In the case of intelligence agencies, they have access to advanced computational resources and may also employ teams of experts in cryptography, making them capable of cracking encryption that would be infeasible for an individual or even most organizations to break. Many encryption algorithms and key lengths currently

---

[31] For an outline, see Layton, R., & Watters, P. A. (2015). Indirect attribution in cyberspace. *Handbook of Research on Digital Crime, Cyberspace Security, and Information Assurance*, 246–262.

used in practice are considered to be secure against even the most powerful adversaries.

Unbreakable encryption is certainly not a new concept, but the internet has bought about scalability challenges. A one-time pad (OTP) is the traditional example making use of a random key. The key is used to encrypt the message, and being symmetric, the inverse is also true. The key is used only once, hence the name one-time pad. And what about quantum cryptography? Fear! Panic?[32]

To encrypt a document using a one-time pad, each character in the source document is paired with a parallel character from the key, and these characters are combined using a bitwise exclusive-or (XOR) operation. This results in a ciphertext document that is completely random and bears no relationship to the source document.

To decrypt the message, the ciphertext message is combined with the key using the same XOR operation. This results in the recovering the original document's contents.

Because the key is truly random and used only once, it is theoretically unbreakable. If the key is kept secret and used only once, the encryption is theoretically unbreakable. However, one-time pads have the drawback of requiring the key to be shared securely and the key size is the same as the message.

Because OTPs are impractical for long-term use or for sending multiple messages, they are typically used in specialized scenarios where the need for unbreakable encryption outweighs the practical difficulties.[33]

Social Engineering

Social engineering Intelligence agencies may use social engineering techniques to gather information or gain access to restricted areas or systems, by tricking people into doing things they shouldn't, or revealing information which should be kept secret.

One example of social engineering used by intelligence agencies is phishing, where a fake email is sent to a user, tricking them into thinking it is legitimate. The user then reveals a username and password, or some other combination of personal data.

Intelligence agencies may also use physical social engineering tactics, such as tailgating (following someone into a restricted area without proper clearance), dumpster diving (looking through trash for sensitive information), or shoulder surfing (watching someone enter a password or PIN).

---

[32] It's coming, for details of the fear and panic, see https://www.infosecurity-magazine.com/opinions/race-quantum-tortoise-beat-hare/

[33] For an overview, see Rubin, F. (1996). One-time pad cryptography. *Cryptologia*, *20*(4), 359–364.

Social engineering can also be used to influence or manipulate groups, such as through propaganda or disinformation campaigns.

It's significant to note that social engineering is not unique to intelligence agencies and can be used by anyone with malicious intent to steal private and personal data.

Artificial Intelligence

Artificial Intelligence (AI) is a versatile and broad set of technologies that try to mimic and/or outperform human intelligence for the counterintelligence mission. Some examples of how intelligence agencies use AI include:

- *Automating data analysis*: AI can be used to reduce complex datasets quickly and easily, following a set of complex rules. This can include analyzing text, images, and videos for insights or identifying patterns and trends.[34]
- *Surveillance and monitoring:* AI can automatically monitor and analyze huge, multiformat datasets, such as social media or satellite imagery, to detect potential threats or track individuals of interest.
- *Language translation*: AI can be used to automatically translate text or speech from one language to another, making it easier for intelligence agencies to understand and analyze information from foreign sources.
- *Predictive analytics*: AI can find regularities and make predictions about potential future events or activities.[35]
- *Cybersecurity*: AI can stop cyber-attacks on an intelligence agency's networks and systems.[36]
- *Improving human decision making*: AI can be used to assist human analysts by providing them with insights, recommendations, and alerts, reducing the time and effort needed to make decisions.

It's significant to note that the use of AI by intelligence agencies raises important ethical considerations, such as issues related to privacy, civil rights, and bias.

---

[34] For a review, see Watters, P. A. (2018). Modelling the Efficacy of Auto-Internet Warnings to Reduce Demand for Child Exploitation Materials. In *Trends and Applications in Knowledge Discovery and Data Mining: PAKDD 2018 Workshops, Revised Selected Papers 22* (pp. 318–329). Springer International Publishing.

[35] For an example, see Watters, P. A., McCombie, S., Layton, R., & Pieprzyk, J. (2012). Characterising and predicting cyber attacks using the Cyber Attacker Model Profile (CAMP). *Journal of Money Laundering Control, 15*(4), 430–441.

[36] For an approach using reasoning and symbolic logic, see Ureche, O., Layton, R., & Watters, P. (2012, October). Towards an implementation of information flow security using semantic web technologies. In *2012 Third Cybercrime and Trustworthy Computing Workshop* (pp. 75–80). IEEE.

Summary

Cyber provides a radical new context for counterintelligence – both dangers and opportunities. Agencies and organizations requiring a counterintelligence function need to be aware of the risks, dangers and limitations – both professional and ethical – before designing a counterintelligence program for the twenty-first century.

Chapter 2
The Cyber Operational Environment

Cybersecurity refers to the practices and technologies used to protect digital systems, networks, and information from unauthorized access, use, disclosure, disruption, modification, or destruction. Some of the key characteristics of cybersecurity include:

- *Confidentiality*: Ensuring that the right people or computers can access sensitive or confidential files or data.
- *Integrity*: Protecting information from unauthorized modification or destruction.
- *Availability*: Ensuring that digital systems and networks are available and accessible when needed.
- *Authentication*: Verifying the identity of users and systems to prevent unauthorized access.[1]
- *Non-repudiation*: Ensuring that the actions of users and systems can be traced and held accountable.
- *Resilience*: Being able to stand up against cybersecurity incidents and recover quickly and effectively.
- *Risk Management*: Identifying and evaluating potential cybersecurity threats, vulnerabilities, and impacts on the organization, and implementing appropriate controls to manage and mitigate risks.
- *Compliance*: Complying with legal and regulatory requirements such as data protection laws and standards like HIPAA, SOX, PCI DSS, etc.
- *Proactivity*: Continuously monitoring and updating the cybersecurity measures to respond to new and evolving threats.

---

[1] For an exhaustive review of identity management practices, frameworks and standards, see Ng, A., Watters, P., & Chen, S. (2014). A Technology and Process Analysis for Contemporary Identity Management Frameworks. In *Inventive Approaches for Technology Integration and Information Resources Management* (pp. 1–52). IGI Global.

- *Collaboration*: Collaborating with other organizations, experts, and government agencies to share information and resources to improve cybersecurity.

Although hacking tends to occupy the headlines, in fact, defensive approaches to cybersecurity can be very effective in practice, when properly planned, executed, and funded. Defensive cybersecurity measures have succeeded in defeating attacks in numerous cases. Some examples include:

- *WannaCry ransomware attack*:[2] In 2017, this piece of malware infected a vast number of hosts worldwide. However, researchers were able to identify a kill switch in the malware that could be activated by registering a specific domain name. This helped to slow the spread of the attack and prevent further damage.
- *Operation Aurora*: In 2009 and 2010, a vast attack targeted corporations like Juniper Networks. The attacks were designed to steal intellectual property and sensitive data. However, companies were able to successfully defend against the attacks by implementing strong security measures, such as two-factor authentication and network segmentation.[3]
- *Mirai botnet*: In 2016, the Mirai botnet disrupted internet services for millions of people through a DDoS attack. However, researchers were able to identify the source code for the botnet and work with law enforcement to take down the infrastructure used to control it.
- *Ukraine power grid attack*: In 2015 and 2016, nefarious hackers thought to be linked to Russia launched a series of attacks on Ukraine's power grid. The attacks caused widespread power outages and disrupted services for millions of people. However, the Ukrainian government was able to restore power relatively quickly by implementing manual overrides and backup systems.[4]

In the counterintelligence context, cybersecurity both from a defensive as well as an operational perspective. That is, cybersecurity provides the means to reveal an adversary's secrets, as well as protecting your own.[5] Cybersecurity program success in counterintelligence – both defensive and offensive – essentially links ICT, physical and personnel security, and classic operational security.

---

[2] For an analysis, see Mohurle, S., & Patil, M. (2017). A brief study of wannacry threat: Ransomware attack 2017. *International Journal of Advanced Research in Computer Science*, 8(5), 1938–1940.

[3] For an insightful analysis, see Alperovitch, D. (2011). *Revealed: operation shady RAT* (Vol. 3, p. 2011). McAfee.

[4] For a review, see Nafees, M. N., Saxena, N., Cardenas, A., Grijalva, S., & Burnap, P. (2023). Smart grid cyber-physical situational awareness of complex operational technology attacks: A review. *ACM Computing Surveys*, 55(10), 1–36.

[5] This definition is adapted from the Australian Signals Directorate motto: "Reveal their secrets. Protect our own"

Defensive Cybersecurity

Regarding counterintelligence, defensive cybersecurity identifies practices and technologies used to stop attacks against digital systems and networks by foreign intelligence services, hackers, and other adversaries. This includes measures such as:

- *Identifying and assessing potential threats*: This includes analyzing the organization's assets and identifying potential vulnerabilities that could be exploited by adversaries.
- *Implementing controls*: This includes implementing technical and administrative controls to protect the organization's assets and reduce vulnerabilities. Examples include firewalls, intrusion detection systems, and access controls.[6]
- *Monitoring*: This includes continuously monitoring the organization's digital systems and networks for signs of unauthorized access or activity.
- *Responding to and recovering from incidents*: Planning to stop breaches[7] or network intrusion. This includes actively planning and practicing response tactics and strategies!
- *Employee education and awareness*: This includes educating employees on the importance of cybersecurity and providing them with training on how to detect and prevent cyber threats.
- *Compliance*: This includes complying with legal and regulatory requirements such as data protection laws and standards like HIPAA, SOX, PCI DSS, etc.
- *Collaboration*: This includes collaborating with other organizations, experts, and government agencies to share information and resources to improve cybersecurity

Defensive cybersecurity measures have supported counterintelligence operations in various cases. One example is the case of Operation Ghost Stories, which was a long-term FBI counterintelligence operation that targeted a group of Russian spies operating in the United States.[8]

In 2010, the FBI discovered that the Russian Foreign Intelligence Service (SVR) had been operating a deep-cover spy ring in the United States for more than a decade. The operation involved a group of Russian operatives living under false identities and using sophisticated spy tradecraft to gather intelligence on U.S. national security interests.

As part of the investigation, the FBI used defensive cybersecurity measures to monitor the suspects' online activity and communications. Specifically, the FBI was

---

[6] For an example, see Watters, P. A., & Ziegler, J. (2016). Controlling information behaviour: the case for access control. *Behaviour & Information Technology*, *35*(4), 268–276.

[7] For an overview of costs, see Layton, R., & Watters, P. A. (2014). A methodology for estimating the tangible cost of data breaches. *Journal of Information Security and Applications*, *19*(6), 321–330.

[8] For an analysis, see Redmond, P. J. (2023). *The Ghost of Angleton: Robert Baer: The Fourth Man: The Hunt for a KGB Spy at the Top of the CIA and the Rise of Putin's Russia* Hachette Books, New York

able to monitor the suspects' use of encrypted communication tools, such as steganography,[9] which allowed them to embed secret messages in seemingly innocuous images.

By monitoring the suspects' online activity, the FBI was able to gather crucial evidence that supported the investigation and ultimately led to the arrest and deportation of the Russian spies. The operation was hailed as a significant success for U.S. counterintelligence efforts and demonstrated the importance of using defensive cybersecurity measures to support intelligence operations.

It's significant that defensive cybersecurity requires continuous review, updating, and adapting to new and evolving threats. Counterintelligence agencies also use defensive cybersecurity measures to protect their own information and systems from foreign intelligence services. One noteworthy example is the case of the NSA and the Shadow Brokers.

In 2016, cybercriminals known as Shadow Brokers began releasing a series of highly classified hacking tools and exploits that they claimed to have stolen from the NSA. The released tools included sophisticated malware, zero-day vulnerabilities, and other exploits that the NSA had used to conduct cyber operations.[10]

The release of these tools was a major embarrassment for the NSA and put its cyber operations at risk. In response, the agency quickly implemented defensive cybersecurity measures to protect itself from further attacks. Specifically, the agency ramped up its monitoring of its own networks and systems to detect any signs of intrusion or unauthorized activity.

The NSA and other agencies helped to identify and patch vulnerabilities in the agency's systems and prevent further leaks of sensitive information.

Offensive Counterespionage

Offensive counterintelligence refers to the proactive measures taken by intelligence agencies and organizations to identify and neutralize foreign intelligence services and other adversaries that are attempting to gather information or conduct espionage against them. These measures can include:

- *Counterintelligence operations*: This includes the use of various techniques to identify and disrupt foreign intelligence services and their agents, such as surveillance, undercover operations, and deception.

---

[9] For an investigation on human limits for detecting steganography, see Watters, P., Martin, F., & Stripf, H. S. (2008). Visual detection of LSB-encoded natural image steganography. *ACM Transactions on Applied Perception (TAP)*, 5(1), 1–12.

[10] For a legal analysis, see Anstis, S., Leonard, N., & Penney, J. W. (2023). Moving from secrecy to transparency in the offensive cyber capabilities sector: The case of dual-use technologies exports. *Computer Law & Security Review*, 48, 105787.

- *Offensive cyber operations*: This includes the use of cyber capabilities to disrupt or compromise foreign intelligence services' networks and systems, such as hacking and malware.
- *Information operations*: This includes the use of various techniques to influence foreign intelligence services and their agents, such as propaganda and disinformation.
- *Protective Security*: This includes the use of various techniques to protect the organization's assets, such as physical security, background checks, security clearances and polygraph examinations.
- *Counter-surveillance*: This includes various techniques uncover foreign intelligence services' surveillance efforts.
- *Counter-intelligence training*: This includes the training of employees, contractors, and other personnel to recognize and report potential espionage activities.
- *Proactive intelligence gathering*: This includes the use of various techniques to gather information on foreign intelligence services and their activities, such as human intelligence and signals intelligence.[11]

Offensive counterintelligence is a high-stakes and high-risk endeavor. It's significant to note that intelligence agencies must operate within the laws and regulations that govern their activities, and any offensive operations must be authorized and supervised by the highest levels of government. There have been some high-profile cases where intelligence agencies have publicly accused foreign governments of conducting cyber espionage activities.

One such case is the indictment of five Chinese military officials by the United States government in 2014 for cyber espionage against American companies. The individuals were were accused of intellectual property crime and stealing other sensitive information from U.S. companies in various industries.[12]

In response to the cyber espionage activities, the U.S. government apparently employed offensive counterespionage measures to disrupt the Chinese hacking group's operations. The exact nature of these measures is not publicly known, but it is believed that they involved a combination of technical and legal tactics.

This case was seen as a significant victory for offensive counterespionage efforts. It sent a clear message to foreign governments that cyber espionage activities would not be tolerated and that there would be consequences for those involved in such activities.

However, there have also been failures and several mixed outcomes. One example is the Stuxnet attack, reportedly involving the U.S. and Israeli governments, described earlier.

---

[11] For a case study on the digital underground, see Lee, S. J., & Watters, P. A. (2016). Gathering intelligence on high-risk advertising and film piracy: A study of the digital underground. *Automating open source intelligence*, 89–102.

[12] To read the case outline, see https://www.fbi.gov/news/stories/five-chinese-military-hackers-charged-with-cyber-espionage-against-us

Stuxnet was a highly sophisticated malware program that targeted Iran's nuclear Supervisory Control and Data Acquisition (SCADA) systems. The malware caused sensitive equipment to burn out, ultimately causing physical damage to the equipment.[13]

While Stuxnet was successful in disrupting Iran's nuclear program, it also had unintended consequences. The malware spread beyond its intended target, infecting thousands of computers around the world. This allowed other countries and non-state actors to study and reverse-engineer the malware, potentially giving them the ability to launch similar attacks in the future.

In addition, the attack also had political consequences. It was seen as an act of aggression by Iran and other countries, and it contributed to a heightened level of tension between Iran and the U.S. and Israel.

Overall, the Stuxnet attack highlights the risks and challenges involved in offensive counterespionage operations in the cyber age. While such operations can be effective in disrupting the activities of foreign governments and protecting national security interests, they can also have unintended consequences and lead to political blowback. It is important for governments to carefully weigh the risks and benefits of such operations and to have strong defensive cybersecurity measures in place to protect against retaliation.

In summary, the case of the Chinese military officials indicted by the U.S. government highlights the importance of offensive counterespionage measures in the cyber age. While the exact tactics used in these operations are often shrouded in secrecy, they can be effective in disrupting the activities of foreign governments and protecting sensitive information from cyber espionage.

Physical and Personnel Security

Personnel security in counterintelligence refers to the measures taken to ensure that individuals working in sensitive positions or with access to sensitive information do not pose a security risk. These measures can include:

- *Background investigations*: This includes conducting thorough background checks on individuals to identify any potential issues such as criminal history, financial problems, foreign contacts, or other factors that could make them vulnerable to foreign intelligence services or other adversaries.
- *Security clearance*: This includes granting access to classified information based on the results of background investigations and other factors such as loyalty, reliability, and need-to-know. Different levels of clearance exist and are granted based on access needs.

---

[13] SCADA! Did someone mention non-existent controls? For a worrying review, see https://www.forbes.com/sites/chuckbrooks/2023/02/15/3-alarming-threats-to-the-us-energy-grid%2D%2Dcyber-physical-and-existential-events/?sh=2feb4d1101a1

- *Polygraph examination*: This includes the use of lie detector tests to verify an individual's trustworthiness and loyalty.
- *Continuous evaluation*: This includes monitoring individuals with access to sensitive information for any changes in behavior or circumstances that could indicate a security risk.
- *Personnel security training*: This includes providing employees, contractors, and other personnel with training on how to recognize and report potential espionage activities.
- *Access controls*: This includes controlling the physical and digital access to sensitive information and facilities by restricting access to only authorized individuals.
- *Exit procedures:* This includes ensuring that employees, contractors, and other personnel who are leaving their positions or have access to sensitive information do not take sensitive information with them and do not pose a security risk.

Personnel security is a critical aspect of counterintelligence as it is the first line of defense against foreign intelligence services and other adversaries. It aims to prevent the compromise of sensitive information by identifying and mitigating any security risks posed by personnel with access to it.

One noteworthy success of personnel security is the case of Reality Winner, who was charged with leaking classified information to the media.[14]

In 2017, Winner printed out a classified document detailing Russian efforts to hack into U.S. election systems and shared it with a news outlet. The document was eventually published, and Winner was quickly identified as the source of the leak.

Winner's arrest and subsequent prosecution were seen as a success for personnel security measures in the cyber age. The investigation into the leak was able to quickly identify and apprehend the perpetrator, and the legal system was able to hold her accountable for her actions.

In addition, the case demonstrated the importance of ongoing personnel security measures to prevent insider threats. In the aftermath of the leak, the NSA implemented new policies and procedures to better monitor and vet contractors, and to limit their access to classified information.

Physical security in counterintelligence suggests a range of protective measures can include:

- *Physical barriers*: This includes the use of walls, fences, gates, and other physical barriers to restrict access to sensitive areas and facilities.
- *Surveillance systems*: This includes the use of cameras, motion detectors, and other surveillance systems to monitor sensitive areas and facilities for any suspicious activity.

---

[14] For an analysis, see https://www.theguardian.com/us-news/2022/jul/25/reality-winner-leaked-file-on-russia-election-hacking-because-public-was-being-lied-to

- *Access controls*: This includes the use of locks, key cards, biometrics, and other means to control access to sensitive areas and facilities by authorized personnel only.
- *Protective measures*: This includes the use of alarms and other detection devices, to prevent damage or destruction of sensitive information and assets.
- *Personnel security*: This includes the use of security personnel, such as guards and patrols, to monitor and secure sensitive areas and facilities.
- *Secure transportation*: This includes the use of secure vehicles, routes, and procedures to transport sensitive information and assets safely and discreetly.
- *Incident response plan*: This includes having a plan in place to respond to security breaches or other incidents, including evacuation procedures and emergency response protocols.
- *Regular security audits*: This includes regularly conducting security audits to identify any vulnerabilities and taking necessary steps to address them.

Physical security is an essential aspect of counterintelligence to protect sensitive information and assets from espionage, terrorism, and cyber-attacks.

Physical security has been successful in supporting counterintelligence in the cyber age by preventing physical access to sensitive information and infrastructure. Here are a few examples:

- *Securing data centers*: Many organizations use physical security measures to secure their data centers, which house critical computing infrastructure and sensitive data. These measures may include biometric authentication, video surveillance, and access controls to prevent unauthorized access to the facility and its contents.
- *Protecting supply chains*: Physical security measures can also be used to protect supply chains, which are increasingly targeted by cyber criminals seeking to steal sensitive information or introduce malware into a system. Organizations may use measures such as secure transportation methods, tamper-evident seals, and on-site inspections to ensure the integrity of their supply chains.[15]
- *Limiting physical access to sensitive information*: Physical security measures can also be used to limit physical access to sensitive information, such as classified documents. For example, organizations may use secure rooms or safes to store classified materials, with access restricted to authorized personnel only.

One example of physical security supporting counterintelligence in the cyber age is the case of the U.S. Department of Defense's (DoD) Joint Strike Fighter (JSF) program.

This is a major defense acquisition program that involves the development and production of advanced fighter aircraft for the U.S. military and its allies. The program has been a target of foreign intelligence services seeking to obtain sensitive information about the aircraft and its technology.

---

[15] The cyber aspects are even more challenging to manage, for details, see https://securitybrief. com.au/story/apac-supply-chains-at-risk-from-cyber-threats-report

To protect against physical theft of sensitive information, the DoD has implemented a range of physical security measures. These measures include secure facilities with restricted access, surveillance cameras, and other security systems.

In 2009, a foreign intelligence service attempted to steal sensitive information about the JSF program by breaking into the computer systems of a defense contractor involved in the program. However, the contractor's physical security measures prevented the attackers from physically gaining access to the computer systems.

The measures in place allowed the contractor to detect the attempted intrusion and quickly respond, preventing the attackers from obtaining any sensitive information. Consequently, the U.S. government was able to stop a potentially devastating loss of sensitive information related to the JSF program.[16]

This case demonstrates the effectiveness of a physical security program against foreign intelligence services.

Operational Security (OPSEC)

Operational security (OPSEC) in counterintelligence are activities that prevent compromise by foreign intelligence services or other adversaries. These measures can include:

- *Information control*: This includes limiting the distribution of sensitive information to only those who have a need-to-know and implementing security measures to protect it.
- *Communication security*: This includes using encryption, secure communication channels, and other measures to protect sensitive information during transmission.
- *Security procedures*: This includes implementing standard operating procedures, such as background checks, security clearance, and personnel security training, to ensure that only those who can be trusted have access to sensitive information.
- *Deception and misdirection*: These include creating false or misleading information to mislead adversaries and conceal sensitive information.
- *Concealment and camouflage*: These include hiding sensitive information and activities from view, such as using cover stories or disguising the true nature of operations.
- *Counterintelligence activities*: This includes identifying, monitoring, and counteracting efforts to gain access to state secrets.
- *Risk management*: This includes identifying potential threats and vulnerabilities and taking steps to mitigate them, such as conducting vulnerability assessments and penetration testing.

---

[16] For further details, see https://thediplomat.com/2015/01/new-snowden-documents-reveal-chinese-behind-f-35-hack/

- *Incident response plan*: This includes having a plan in place to respond to security breaches or other incidents, including evacuation procedures and emergency response protocols.

One example of how OPSEC supported counterintelligence in the cyber age is the case of the CIA's communications with assets in China.

In 2010, the Chinese government reportedly launched a major operation against the CIA's assets in China; several CIA agents were sent to jail. The operation was reportedly enabled by the compromise of the CIA's communications systems, which allowed the Chinese government to intercept and decode the agency's communications with its assets.[17]

Following the compromise, the CIA implemented several OPSEC measures to better protect its communications with assets. These measures included the use of more secure communication channels, such as in-person meetings and encrypted messaging applications, as well as novel communication protocols.

As a result of these OPSEC measures, the CIA was able to rebuild its communications with assets in China and prevent further losses. The agency also reportedly developed new techniques for detecting and countering compromise of its communications systems, including the use of advanced encryption and other security technologies.

This case demonstrates the importance of operational security measures in protecting against compromise of communications systems and maintaining the security of sensitive information. By implementing strong OPSEC measures, organizations can better protect against insider threats, surveillance, and other forms of compromise.

Operational security is an essential aspect of counterintelligence as it aims to protect sensitive information and activities from being discovered or compromised by foreign intelligence services or other adversaries. It is important to have a strong operational security plan in place to stop security breaches.

Summary

The twenty-first century has seen the evolution of threats and responses in the field; they are many and varied, including the following:

- The growing use of technology: As more and more organizations and individuals rely on technology; the number of potential vulnerabilities and attack surfaces increases.

---

[17] For an outline of events, see https://www.nytimes.com/2017/05/20/world/asia/china-cia-spies-espionage.html

- The increasing sophistication of cyber threats: Adversaries are becoming more sophisticated and are using a range of techniques to evade detection and gain access to sensitive information.
- The evolving threat landscape: new technologies and new forms of communication have created new opportunities for adversaries to hack hosts.
- The challenge of protecting against insider threats: Insiders, whether malicious or negligent.
- The challenge of protecting against Advanced Persistent Threats (APTs) created and disseminated by nation-states.
- The challenge of protecting against social engineering: Stopping staff from revealing information they should not disclose.
- The challenge of protecting against supply chain attacks: Adversaries are increasingly targeting suppliers and other third-party vendors.

To solve these challenges, organizations and individuals must adopt a multi-layered approach to security that includes cybersecurity, counterintelligence, and operational security measures.

The operational environment provides numerous challenges for counterintelligence practitioners. However, by combining a standards-references approach with pragmatic tradecraft adapted from traditional approaches, an effective strategy can be developed and implemented.

Chapter 3
Cyber Threats (and Opportunities)

The same cybersecurity activities that pose a threat to one's own organization are also the source of opportunity for offensive counterintelligence. This seeming paradox makes the deep study of cyber tactics critically important for counterintelligence professionals. In this chapter, the key attack vectors for cybersecurity operations are described from both an offensive and a defensive perspective.

The most common attack vectors include:

- *Phishing*: The use of fraudulent messages to get staff to reveal confidential data about themselves, including login usernames and password.
- *Ransomware*: Malware that extorts the user into paying a ransom, either through crypto-ransomware or exfiltration followed by a data breach.[1]
- *Malware*: Malicious software that includes viruses, worms, and Trojans.
- *Hacking*: Attempts to break into systems or networks.
- *Distributed Denial of Service (DDoS) attacks*: Flooding a website or network with traffic in order to overload it and make it unavailable.
- *Advanced Persistent Threats (APTs):* nation-states working hard over time to develop new technologies that can help them "get root".
- *Social engineering*: Tricking individuals into revealing sensitive information or providing access to systems.
- *Supply chain attacks*: Targeting suppliers and other third-party vendors to reveal confidential data.
- *IoT attacks*: Exploiting vulnerabilities in IoT devices.
- *Cloud attacks*: Exploiting weaknesses in the cloud and virtualized infrastructure to break into systems.

---

[1] For a review, see McIntosh, T., Kayes, A. S. M., Chen, Y. P. P., Ng, A., & Watters, P. (2021). Dynamic user-centric access control for detection of ransomware attacks. *Computers & Security*, *111*, 102461.

P. A. Watters, *Counterintelligence in a Cyber World*,
https://doi.org/10.1007/978-3-031-35287-4_3

Significantly, these are just examples, with new attack vectors are constantly emerging as technology evolves, and cyber attackers become more sophisticated. A comprehensive cyber defense strategy should include not only the protection against known attack vectors but also the ability to detect and respond to new and emerging threats.

One example that tied a number of these attack vectors together was the 2021 attack on the Colonial Pipeline, which provides nearly half of the fuel supply for the U.S. East Coast.[2]

The attack began with a successful phishing email that tricked an employee into providing their credentials, which the attackers then used to hack a range of hosts. DarkSide ransomware then proceeded to encrypt data on these hosts, and extortion followed closely.

The attackers also used social engineering tactics to further their attack. They reportedly threatened to leak the stolen data to the public and used fake data leak sites to put pressure on the company to pay the ransom. The attackers also targeted Colonial Pipeline's industrial control systems, which are used to manage the flow of fuel through the pipeline, potentially putting public safety at risk.

The attack caused widespread disruption to the fuel supply chain, leading to shortages and price spikes across the East Coast. The incident also highlighted the growing threat of ransomware attacks and the importance of strong cybersecurity defenses, including employee training and incident response planning.

This case study demonstrates how cyber attackers can use a combination of phishing, ransomware, and social engineering tactics to launch highly effective attacks against even critical infrastructure. It also underscores the importance of proactive cybersecurity measures, including employee training, incident response planning, and strong access controls, in preventing and mitigating consequences.

From a counterintelligence perspective, while disruption and sabotage may form part of an offensive program, an undisclosed or undetected data breach is probably the most typical tactic. Breaches can happen through physical means such as the loss or theft of unencrypted laptops, smartphones, or backup tapes containing personal data, as well as the more obvious vectors of attack.

The types of information that may be involved in a data breach include personal identification numbers (PINs), login credentials and other personal information. A data breach may also occur through a loss of control over sensitive data, such as when an employee accidentally sends an email containing sensitive information to the wrong recipient.

---

[2] To read the full business case summary, see Hobbs, A. (2021). The colonial pipeline hack: Exposing vulnerabilities in us cybersecurity. In *SAGE Business Cases*. SAGE Publications: SAGE Business Cases Originals.

Data Breaches

Data breaches can result in identity theft, fraud, and other types of cybercrime. Organizations that experience data breaches are often required to notify affected individuals and regulatory agencies and may face fines and other penalties.

Intelligence agencies may target and collect a wide range of data, depending on their specific mission and objectives. This can include:

- *Personal information*: all of the obvious personal data points, including highly prized data such as passport numbers.
- *Financial data*: including payment and transaction records.
- *Communications data*: such as email, text messages, and phone call records.
- *Location data*: such as GPS coordinates, IP addresses, and travel itineraries.
- *Biometric data*: such as fingerprints, facial recognition data, and DNA samples.
- *Documents*: especially if related to government, military, and political activities. This can include classified documents, diplomatic cables, and information on weapons systems and military operations.
- *Industrial and commercial data*: such as intellectual property and financial performance data of companies.
- *Social media data*: such as posts, likes, and personal data of users.

The largest data breach in US history was the 2017 Equifax data breach,[3] which exposed the names, birth dates, and credit card numbers, as well as a plethora of other personal data for thousands of users.

The breach could have been used to support counterintelligence efforts in several ways. For example, foreign intelligence services could use the stolen data to identify and target specific individuals for recruitment as assets or for blackmail. The data could also be used to gain insights into the financial and employment status of US government employees or contractors, which could be used to target them for additional intelligence gathering.

Additionally, the breach highlights the importance of protecting personal and sensitive data from cyber-attacks. The failure to secure such information could put national security at risk by enabling foreign intelligence services to gain access to sensitive information and target individuals for recruitment or blackmail.

In the wake of the Equifax breach, the US government has taken steps to strengthen cybersecurity and protect against future attacks, including increasing funding for cybersecurity initiatives, expanding partnerships with the private sector, and developing new regulations and standards for protecting sensitive data.

It's important to note that intelligence agencies may also use AI and related technologies to recover patterns and connections that would be difficult for humans to discern. This is covered further in Chap. 8.

---

[3] For a review, see Gressin, S. (2017). The equifax data breach: What to do. *Federal Trade Commission, 8.*

Malware

Malware (short for malicious software) can be used for intelligence gathering in several ways, such as:

- *Remote Access Trojans (RATs)*: These types of malware allows an attacker to control an infected device, exfiltrate data, and monitor the victim's activities.
- *Keyloggers*: This type of malware records all keystrokes on an infected device, allowing an attacker to record personal data.
- *Data exfiltration malware*: specific types of data, such as documents and files, can be stolen and sent to the attacker.
- *Network reconnaissance malware*: This type of malware can be used to map out the victim's network, identify other devices connected to it, and potentially gain access to additional systems.
- *Advanced persistent threat (APT) malware*: This type of malware permits the attacker to steal data, and maintain access to hosts.
- *Rootkits*: Rootkits are designed to hide the presence of other malware and to conceal the attacker's actions on the target machine.
- *Botnets*: collections of compromised hosts that can be coordinated by a hacker to carry out various DDoS attacks.

It's important to note that malware can be used to gather various type of data, and intelligence agencies can use different types of malware depending on their targets and objectives.[4]

Some examples of highly complex malware include:[5]

- *Flame*: Discovered in 2012, Flame is a highly sophisticated and complex malware that targeted systems in the Middle East, particularly Iran. Flame was designed to gather information and data from infected systems, including screenshots, audio recordings, and keyboard activity.
- *Duqu*: Discovered in 2011, Duqu is a highly sophisticated Trojan horse malware that was used for cyber espionage. Duqu was designed to steal sensitive data from infected systems, including information related to industrial control systems.
- *Gauss*: Discovered in 2012, Gauss is a highly sophisticated malware that was designed to steal banking credentials and other sensitive data from infected systems. Gauss is also capable of collecting information on infected systems, including browser history and cookies.
- *Regin*: Discovered in 2014, Regin is a highly sophisticated malware that has been used for cyber espionage and intelligence gathering. Regin can perform a wide

---

[4] For a review of technical countermeasures, see McIntosh, T., Watters, P., Kayes, A. S. M., Ng, A., & Chen, Y. P. P. (2021). Enforcing situation-aware access control to build malware-resilient file systems. *Future Generation Computer Systems*, *115*, 568–582.

[5] For details of these samples and others, see Bencsáth, B., Pék, G., Buttyán, L., & Felegyhazi, M. (2012). The cousins of stuxnet: Duqu, flame, and gauss. *Future Internet*, *4*(4), 971–1003

range of functions, including stealing data, taking screenshots, and logging keystrokes.

For malware design to facilitate surveillance, three key factors are essential:

- *Stealth*: For malware to be effective for surveillance, it must be able to evade detection by antivirus and other security software. This can be achieved through techniques such as code obfuscation, anti-debugging, and anti-tampering, and novel delivery mechanisms, such as advertising.[6]
- *Persistence*: The malware can gain a foothold on the target's hosts even after the initial compromise. This can be achieved through rootkits, bootkits, and can survive system reboots and software updates.
- *Capabilities*: The malware must be able to gather and transmit the desired information from the target's system. The malware must have the ability to record keystrokes, take screenshots, capture audio and video, and exfiltrate data, etc. It must also be able to bypass firewalls and other security measures and maintain a connection to the command and control servers.

These factors are critical to the success of malware designed for surveillance because they enable the malware to evade detection and remain on the target's system for an extended period, while also gathering and transmitting the desired information.

One example of malware being used for surveillance is the Hacking Team Remote Control System (RCS) malware. Hacking Team was an Italian company that specialized in the development of surveillance tools and was known to cooperate with agencies and policing organizations globally.[7]

The Hacking Team RCS malware was designed to allow its users to remotely monitor and control targeted devices, including computers and mobile phones. The malware was highly sophisticated and could be customized to suit the specific needs of its users.

In 2015, an attack against Hacking Team allowed the public release of the company's internal documents, including source code and user manuals for its RCS malware. The leaked documents revealed that the malware was being used by various government agencies and law enforcement organizations in Egypt and Saudi Arabia.

The Hacking Team RCS malware allowed monitoring of activities on targeted devices, including email and chat, as well as location data and keystrokes. It also had the ability to remotely activate a device's camera and microphone, allowing its users to capture audio and video recordings.

---

[6] For a case study, see Herps, A., Watters, P. A., & Pineda-Villavicencio, G. (2013). Measuring Surveillance in Online Advertising: A Big Data Approach. In *2013 Fourth Cybercrime and Trustworthy Computing Workshop* (pp. 30–35). IEEE.

[7] For details, see Marquis-Boire, M., Scott-Railton, J., Guarnieri, C., Kleemola, K., Technica, K. S. T., Gear, S., ... & Kennedys, D. (2012). Police Story: Hacking Team's Government Surveillance Malware. *Citizen Lab. University of Toronto. Archived from the original on 25 June 2014. Retrieved 3 August 2014.*

The use of Hacking Team's RCS malware for surveillance purposes raised significant privacy concerns, and the company faced criticism for its business practices. The leak of the company's internal documents resulted in the loss of valuable intellectual property and damaged the reputation of the company. The incident highlights the need for strong cybersecurity measures and responsible business practices in the development and deployment of surveillance tools.

Phishing

Phishing is a common tactic used in counterintelligence to compromise a target's computer systems through the human factor. Phishing can be used in the following ways:

- *Spear-phishing*: This phishing in which an attacker sends a personalized greeting to a specific individual or organization, often using information gathered from social media or other sources.
- *Whaling*: This type of phish targets politicians or business leaders.
- *Baiting*: this is a form of phishing in which the attacker offers something that the victim wants, like a free software, service, or a valuable item, to gain access to sensitive information.
- *Vishing*: uses phone calls or voicemails to trick the victim.
- *Smishing*: as above, but for texting.
- *Pharming*: This type of phishing tricks the victim into visiting a fake website that looks like a legitimate one, to steal sensitive information.

Counterintelligence agencies may use these methods to target individuals or organizations, to gain access to that information or to install malware on their systems.

It's important to note that phishing attacks can be very sophisticated, and it's hard for the victims to detect, and it's one of the most common attack vectors used by cybercriminals and state-sponsored actors.

One example of phishing being used for intelligence gathering is the "Operation Pawn Storm" campaign.[8] Operation Pawn Storm is believed to be a state-sponsored cyber espionage group that has been active since at least 2007, and has been linked to various attacks targeting government, military, and media organizations around the world.

One of the techniques used by Operation Pawn Storm is phishing, where attackers send emails with malicious attachments or links that, when clicked, install malware on the victim's computer or steal sensitive information. Operation Pawn Storm has been known to use highly sophisticated and convincing phishing emails that are tailored to the specific interests and activities of their targets.

---

[8] For a review, see Hacquebord, F. (2017). Two years of pawn storm. *Trend Micro Forward-Looking Threat Research Team*.

In one case, Operation Pawn Storm targeted the German Parliament (Bundestag) with a phishing campaign in 2015. The attackers sent emails that appeared to be from the United Nations, with links to fake websites that mimicked the UN's official site. The fake websites were designed to steal login credentials from Bundestag employees and gain access to the organization's internal network.

The phishing campaign was successful. They were then able to move laterally through the network and steal sensitive information, including confidential emails and documents. The attack was only discovered after several months, and it was found that the attackers had been inside the network for nearly a year.

The Operation Pawn Storm campaign demonstrates the effectiveness of phishing as a technique for intelligence gathering and highlights the need for strong cybersecurity measures and employee education to prevent these types of attacks.

System and Network Penetration

System and network penetration can be used in counterintelligence as a means of gaining unauthorized access to sensitive information or to compromise a target's computer systems. This type of activity can be used in the following ways:

- *Vulnerability scanning*: finding open ports and other weaknesses in a target's systems or networks. This information can be used to identify potential points of entry for an attack.
- *Exploit development*: Once vulnerabilities have been identified, attackers may develop custom exploits to take advantage of them, including malware installation.
- *Remote access*: Once an attacker has gained access to a target's systems, they may use remote access tools to control the compromised systems and exfiltrate data.
- *Persistence*: maintaining access to the target's systems even after an initial compromise. This can be achieved through the use of backdoors, rootkits, or other types of malware.
- *Network reconnaissance*: This is the process of gathering information about a target's network, such as identifying other systems connected to it and mapping out the network's structure.
- *Lateral movement*: This means moving from one compromised system to another within a target's network, to compromise additional systems.
- *Data exfiltration*: This is the process of stealing sensitive information from a target's systems and transmitting it to the attacker.

These types of activities are typically used by intelligence agencies and other advanced threat actors to compromise hosts and networks.

A well-known example of an Israeli cyber-attack to defeat intelligence gathering is the 2014 cyber-attack against the Lebanese militant group Hezbollah.

In 2014, the Israeli Defense Forces (IDF) launched a cyber-attack against Hezbollah's computer networks. The attack was part of a wider Israeli campaign to disrupt Hezbollah's operations and reduce its military capabilities.[9]

The attack reportedly involved the use of malicious software to target and disrupt Hezbollah's communications and logistics networks. The malware was able to infiltrate the networks and cause significant disruption, including the loss of valuable intelligence data.

The attack was seen as a significant success for the Israeli military, as it demonstrated the potential of cyber warfare to disrupt and weaken enemy organizations. It also highlighted the importance of defensive cyber security measures, to stop these types of attacks.

Summary

Malware, phishing, and related cyber tactics are commonly used for offensive operations. Developing defensive strategies to uncover their use – and potentially identify inside sponsorship or enablement – are key requirements for any counterintelligence function.

---

[9] For a review, see Saressalo, T. J. (2019). Israeli Defense Forces' Information Operations 2006–2014, Part 1. *Journal of Information Warfare*, *18*(1), 87–102.

Chapter 4
Psychology and Criminal Profiling

What makes a key staff member vulnerable to psychological pressure? What motivates people to reveal state secrets or proprietary information? Unpacking the psychology around espionage is critically important when looking at the intersection of behavior and the tools which cybersecurity provides.

There are several factors that can make people vulnerable to psychological pressure in espionage:

- *Financial difficulties*: People who are facing financial difficulties may be more willing to accept money in exchange for sensitive information.
- *Emotional vulnerability*: People who are going through a difficult time in their personal lives, such as a breakup or the loss of a loved one, may be more susceptible to emotional manipulation.
- *Sense of adventure*: Some individuals may be drawn to the excitement and thrill of espionage and may be more willing to take risks.
- *Ideological beliefs*: People who are passionate about a certain cause or ideology may be more likely to be recruited by groups that align with their beliefs.
- *Lack of loyalty*: People who do not feel strongly committed to their organization or country may be more susceptible to recruitment by foreign intelligence services.
- *Lack of security awareness*: People who are not aware of the risks of espionage and the methods that are used to recruit individuals may be more susceptible to psychological pressure.
- *Ego*: Some people may be more susceptible to flattery and may be more willing to provide information to someone who they perceive as important or powerful.[1]
- *Trust*: People who are trustworthy are more vulnerable to psychological pressure as they may not suspect any malicious intent.

---

[1] Your goose could be easily cooked! For a case, see https://theconversation.com/you-could-break-espionage-laws-on-social-media-without-realising-it-151665

These factors can make people more susceptible to recruitment by foreign intelligence services and more vulnerable to psychological pressure tactics that are often used in espionage. To understand why these factors are important, it's important to investigate the underlying individual and group processes which may influence bad decision making, including motivation models, personality, cognition, and links to mood and stress.

Also, psychological pressure can be exerted at the national scale, affecting many individuals, but primarily as a group, across any one of these dimensions. One example of an intelligence agency exploiting financial vulnerabilities in the cyber age is the case of the North Korea.

In 2017, the United States government announced a new strategy for the atomic war program in North Korea, which included imposing economic sanctions on the country. As part of this strategy, the US government worked with international partners to disrupt North Korea's access to the global financial system.[2]

One of the key tools used in this effort was cyber operations designed to target and disrupt North Korea's financial activities. For example, in 2018, the US Department of Justice indicted several North Korean individuals who were accused of attacking a Bangladeshi bank that resulted in losses of $81 million.

The US government has also been working to disrupt North Korea's use of cryptocurrencies, which are seen as a potential means of circumventing financial sanctions. In 2019, the US Department of the Treasury announced new sanctions targeting two Chinese nationals who were accused of helping North Korea to launder cryptocurrency transactions.

The US government's efforts to exploit financial vulnerabilities in North Korea highlight the increasing importance of cyber operations in modern intelligence gathering and counterintelligence activities. By disrupting financial activities, intelligence agencies can not only weaken the enemy's ability to fund their operations but also gain valuable insights into their financial networks and operations.

Motivation

There are several theories of motivation, but some of the most widely recognized and studied include:[3]

- *Maslow's Hierarchy of Needs*: an individual must satisfy lower-level needs (like eating) before satisfying higher level ones, such as self-actualization.
- *Alderfer's ERG theory*: Focuses on the three dimensions of existence, relatedness, and growth.

---

[2] For details, see Zakharova, L. (2019). The influence of UN security council sanctions on the North Korean economy. *International Organisations Research Journal, 14*(2), 223–244.

[3] For specific links to cyber, see Bada, M., Sasse, A. M., & Nurse, J. R. (2019). Cyber security awareness campaigns: Why do they fail to change behaviour?. *arXiv preprint arXiv:1901.02672.*

- *Herzberg's Two-Factor Theory*: Motivation comes from hygiene and motivators.
- *Expectancy Theory*: Ensuring that outcomes anticipated match the input and effort required to achieve what is desired.
- *Self-Efficacy Theory*: states that an individual's belief in their ability to perform a task is a major determinant of their motivation to engage in that task.

These are some of the most well-known and widely studied theories of motivation, but there are also other theories such as the Goal Setting theory, the Attribution theory, the Self-Perception theory, etc.

The case of Harold Martin is illustrative of the potential - a former NSA contractor who was convicted of stealing classified information in 2019. Martin was motivated to steal the information by a desire for recognition and validation.[4]

According to reports, Martin began stealing classified information in 2015, shortly after experiencing personal and professional setbacks. At the time, Martin was struggling with basic physiological and safety needs, including financial instability and job insecurity.

However, Martin was also motivated by higher-level needs, such as the need for recognition and validation. Martin had a history of feeling undervalued and overlooked at work, and he believed that stealing classified information would give him a sense of importance and validation.

This case study highlights how motivational theory can be used to explain why individuals engage in espionage or other forms of intelligence activities, even in the cyber age. By addressing both basic needs and higher-level needs such as recognition and validation, intelligence agencies can better understand and prevent espionage and other forms of insider threats.

Motivational theory can be further related to counterintelligence in several ways:

- Understanding what motivates people to engage in espionage can help counterintelligence agencies identify potential spies and develop strategies to prevent them from carrying out their activities. For example, if people are to engage in espionage by a desire for power, counterintelligence agencies can focus on identifying individuals who have a strong desire for power and may be more susceptible to recruitment by foreign intelligence services.
- Identifying what motivates people to be loyal to their country and their organization can help counterintelligence agencies protect their own personnel from recruitment by foreign intelligence services. For example, if people want to be loyal to their country and organization by a sense of belonging and identification, counterintelligence agencies can focus on creating an organizational culture that promotes a sense of belonging and identification.
- Exploring what motivates people to report suspicious activities can help counterintelligence agencies develop strategies to encourage employees to report any suspicious activity that may indicate espionage. For example, if people are

---

[4] For a summary, see Shane, S. (2019). NSA Contractor Admits Guilt Over Stolen Secrets. *The New York Times*, A15-L.

encouraged to report suspicious activity by a sense of civic duty, counterintelligence agencies can focus on creating an organizational culture that promotes a sense of civic duty and encourages employees to report suspicious activities.

- Determining the psychological pressures and methods used by foreign intelligence services to influence and compromise individuals can help counterintelligence agencies to develop effective countermeasures, such as counter-surveillance techniques, counterpropaganda and de-radicalization, to protect individuals and organizations from these pressures.
- Assessing how to create a motivated workforce that is highly engaged in the protection of their country and their organization is important for counterintelligence agencies as it can enhance the ability to detect and prevent espionage activities.

One case study for how reporting suspicious activities can help counterintelligence agencies is the Ana Montes case arrested for espionage in 2001.[5]

Montes had been working for the DIA for over a decade and had access to classified information about US military operations in Latin America. Despite her high-level security clearance, Montes was able to pass sensitive information to the Cuban government for years without being detected.

In 1996, Montes was observed acting suspiciously by a coworker who reported her behavior to DIA authorities. The coworker had noticed that Montes was spending an unusual amount of time studying maps of Latin America and was making frequent phone calls to a suspicious number. These behaviors raised red flags for the coworker, who reported them to superiors.

As a result of the coworker's report, DIA authorities began investigating Montes and eventually uncovered her involvement in espionage. Montes received a sentence of 25 years in prison.

This case study highlights the importance of reporting suspicious activities to counterintelligence agencies. By being vigilant and reporting suspicious behavior, individuals can help prevent espionage and other forms of insider threats. Counterintelligence agencies rely on the cooperation of the public to identify potential threats and protect national security.

In summary, motivational theory can provide counterintelligence agencies with insight into people's behavior and decision-making, which can be used to identify potential threats, protect personnel and organizations, and promote a culture of security.

---

[5] For details, see De La Cova, A. (2007). True Believer: Inside the Investigation and Capture of Ana Montes, Cuba's Master Spy: Carmichael, Scott W.: Annapolis: Naval Institute Press, 187 pp., Publication Date: March 2007.

Personality Theories

There are many personality theories, but some of the most studied and well-known include:[6]

- The Five Factor Model (FFM) or the "Big Five" personality traits deriving from Openness, Conscientiousness, Extraversion, Agreeableness, and Neuroticism.
- The Myers-Briggs Type Indicator (MBTI) is a theory that suggests that people fit into one of 16 personality types based on their preferences for Extraversion vs. Introversion, Sensing vs. Intuition, Thinking vs. Feeling, and Judging vs. Perceiving.
- The Trait theory, which suggests that personality is made up of several different traits that are relatively stable across time.
- The psychoanalytic theory, which suggests that personality is determined by unconscious conflicts and desires, and that childhood experiences play a major role in shaping adult personality.
- The Social Cognitive theory, which suggests that personality is shaped by the interaction between the individual, their environment, and their behavior.
- The Self-Regulation theory, which suggests that people can regulate their thoughts, emotions, and behavior in order to meet their goals and objectives.

These theories provide different perspectives on the nature of personality and the factors that contribute to its development and expression. One case study for how social cognitive theory has supported counterintelligence operations is the case of "Operation Ghost Stories," a counterintelligence operation conducted by the FBI in 2010.[7]

The operation targeted Russian agents who had been living in the United States for several years under false identities. These agents had been trained by Russian intelligence agencies to blend in with American society and gather information for the Russian government.

The FBI was able to uncover the network through a combination of traditional counterintelligence techniques, such as surveillance and wiretapping, as well as the application of social cognitive theory.

The role of social influences and learning in shaping behavior is predicted by social cognition theory. In the case of the Russian sleeper agents, the FBI used this theory to understand how the agents had been trained to think and behave in a way that would allow them to blend in with American society. By understanding the agents' social and cultural background, the FBI was able to predict their behavior and identify patterns that could be used to track their activities.

---

[6] For applications in cyber specifically, see McBride, M., Carter, L., & Warkentin, M. (2012). Exploring the role of individual employee characteristics and personality on employee compliance with cybersecurity policies. *RTI International-Institute for Homeland Security Solutions*, 5(1), 1.

[7] For details, see Faou, M., Tartare, M., & Dupuy, T. (2019). Operation ghost. *ESET Research White papers, October 2019.*

For example, the FBI monitored the agents' use of certain phrases and terminology that was unique to their training. They also observed their use of certain technologies, such as encrypted communication channels, which were consistent with the training they had received from Russian intelligence agencies.

Through a combination of traditional and social cognitive techniques, the FBI was able to identify and arrest the Russian sleeper agents. The case study highlights the importance of using social cognitive theory to understand the behavior of individuals involved in espionage and other forms of counterintelligence.

Personality theory can be used to improve counterintelligence in several ways. Some examples include:

- *Identifying potential vulnerabilities*: By understanding the personality traits and characteristics that are associated with susceptibility to persuasion and manipulation, counterintelligence professionals can better identify and protect individuals who may be at risk of being targeted by foreign intelligence agencies.
- *Understanding motivations*: By understanding the motivations that drive individuals to engage in espionage or other forms of disloyal behavior, counterintelligence professionals can better anticipate and prevent such activities from occurring.
- *Profiling*: By profiling individuals who are suspected of being involved in espionage or other forms of disloyal behavior, counterintelligence professionals can better understand their behavior and anticipate their next moves.[8]
- *Developing Interrogation techniques*: By understanding the psychological needs of individuals, counterintelligence professionals can develop more effective and humane methods of interrogation and debriefing.
- *Developing countermeasures*: By understanding the personality traits and characteristics of people at risk of espionage or other forms of disloyal behavior, counterintelligence professionals can develop more effective countermeasures to prevent such activities from occurring.
- *Improving recruitment and vetting*: By understanding the personality traits and characteristics that are associated with loyalty and trustworthiness, counterintelligence professionals can improve the recruitment and vetting of individuals who will have access to sensitive information. Theory could be used to develop better recruitment procedures, training programs and countermeasures to identify, deter and prevent espionage activities.

A case for how personality theory has supported counterintelligence operations is the case of Joshua Adam Schulte, a former CIA employee who was arrested in 2018

---

[8] As outlined in Chap. 8, pattern recognition can also be deployed to assist in profiling, for a case study, see Perez, C., Birregah, B., Layton, R., Lemercier, M., & Watters, P. (2013, August). REPLOT: retrieving profile links on twitter for suspicious networks detection. In *Proceedings of the 2013 IEEE/ACM International Conference on Advances in Social Networks Analysis and Mining* (pp. 1307–1314).

for stealing and transmitting classified national defense information to an organization believed to be WikiLeaks.[9]

According to court documents, Schulte was described by his former colleagues as a "disgruntled employee" who had a history of erratic behavior, including anger issues, alcohol abuse, and difficulty working with others. These personality traits likely contributed to his decision to steal and leak classified information, as well as his efforts to cover up his involvement in the crime.

Counterintelligence investigators reportedly used personality assessments and psychological profiling to help identify Schulte as a potential suspect, as well as to gain insights into his motivations, mindset, and behavior patterns. This information was used to build a case against him and ultimately secure his arrest and conviction.

In summary, personality theory can provide counterintelligence professionals with valuable insights into the behavior, motivations, and vulnerabilities of individuals who may be involved in espionage or other forms of disloyal behavior, which can help them to better protect national security.[10]

Cognition

How people process information is critical to identifying how to best create an approach, whether that is through a spear phishing message or something more sophisticated.[11] There are several major theories of cognition, including:

- *Connectionism*: This theory proposes that cognition arises from the interactions between simple processing units, such as neurons, and the patterns of connections between them.
- *Symbolic processing*: This theory proposes that cognition arises from the manipulation of symbols, such as words or numbers, in a rule-based system.
- *Information processing*: A theory that proposes that cognition can be understood as the processing of information through a series of stages, such as perception, attention, and memory.
- *Social cognitive theory*: This theory proposes that cognitive processes are shaped by the social and cultural contexts in which individuals operate, and that

---

[9] For a summary, see Heubl, B. (2021). Profile update for the modern SPY. *Engineering & Technology, 16*(9), 1–5.

[10] For an example involving profiling online offenders, see Watters, P. A., Lueg, C., Spiranovic, C., & Prichard, J. (2013). Patterns of ownership of child model sites: Profiling the profiteers and consumers of child exploitation material. *First Monday*.

[11] For national security applications, see Regens, J. L. (2019). Augmenting human cognition to enhance strategic, operational, and tactical intelligence. *Intelligence and National Security, 34*(5), 673–687.

individuals also use cognitive processes to navigate and make sense of those contexts.[12]

- *Dynamic systems theory*: This theory proposes that cognition arises from the interactions and feedback loops between different cognitive, neural, and physiological processes.
- *Embodied cognition*: This theory proposes that cognition is deeply rooted in the body and the physical interactions with the world.

Each of these theories offers a unique perspective on how cognitive processes work, and their consequences. An understanding of cognition can assist counterintelligence by providing insight into how individuals and groups think, process information, and make decisions. This can be predict potential vulnerabilities, as well as to develop more effective countermeasures and strategies for protecting against espionage and other forms of intelligence gathering. In addition, understanding the cognitive processes that influence decision-making, such as biases and heuristics, can help counterintelligence professionals to identify and neutralize disinformation and other forms of disinformation.

A relevant case study for how cognitive theory has supported counterintelligence operations is the case of a Chinese national named Yanjun Xu. According to court documents, Xu was a senior official in China's Ministry of State Security (MSS) and was responsible for targeting and recruiting employees of US aviation and aerospace companies to steal trade secrets and other sensitive information. To carry out these operations, Xu and his colleagues used various cognitive techniques, such as social engineering, phishing, and other forms of deception, to gain the trust of their targets and convince them to share information.[13]

Counterintelligence investigators reportedly used cognitive theories and techniques to gain insights into Xu's methods and motivations, as well as to develop countermeasures to protect US companies and employees from similar attacks. This included analyzing patterns of behavior and cognitive biases, developing training programs to help employees identify and respond to phishing and social engineering attacks, and building stronger partnerships with the private sector to share intelligence and coordinate response efforts.

---

[12] Subcultural aspects also need to be considered, especially in the cybercrime context. For an example, see Prichard, J., Spiranovic, C., Watters, P., & Lueg, C. (2013). Young people, child pornography, and subcultural norms on the Internet. *Journal of the American Society for Information Science and Technology, 64*(5), 992–1000.

[13] For a case study, see Schnell, J. (2022). Cultural Variables Within Prosecution of Chinese Corporate Espionage: The Case of USA Versus Yanjun Xu. *Fudan Journal of the Humanities and Social Sciences, 15*(4), 501–512.

Stress and Mood

Stress is a necessary part of life, ensuring that people can respond appropriately to physical or emotional challenges. It can be excessive, and can be triggered by events or situations, including work, relationships, and health issues.

Mood refers to a person's emotional condition. It is a broad term that encompasses feelings such as happiness, sadness, anger, and anxiety. Mood can be affected by a wide range of factors, including stress, but it can also be influenced by other factors such as genetics, personality, and life experiences. Mood can also vary over time, and people can experience changes in mood as a normal part of life.

Stress can also affect mood, and mood can affect stress. Stressful situations can cause feelings of anxiety, worry, and sadness, and these feelings can, in turn, make it more difficult to cope with stress. On the other hand, positive mood associated with happiness and contentment can make stress more manageable.

When a person is under stress or experiencing negative mood they may be more likely to make poor decisions, be less vigilant, or be more susceptible to manipulation. Stress can also make people more likely to act impulsively or recklessly, which can make them more susceptible to exploitation by intelligence agents. Negative mood can also lead to feelings of hopelessness or despair, which can make it harder for a person to resist the advances of an intelligence agent.

In addition, people who are struggling with stress or negative mood may be more likely to seek out support or companionship, which can make them more vulnerable to recruitment or manipulation by an intelligence agent posing as a friend or confidant.

In contrast, positive mood and well-being can make people more resilient to the influence of intelligence agents. When people feel good about themselves and their situation, they are less likely to be swayed by manipulation, and they are more likely to be able to identify and resist attempts at recruitment or influence.

It's also important to note that intelligence agencies sometimes use psychological techniques to exploit vulnerabilities in their targets, these techniques are known as "influence operations" or "covert action" and may involve psychological profiling, manipulation, and deception.

The case of Glenn Duffie Shriver is relevant here; Shriver was a former college student recruited by Chinese intelligence to gather information on US officials.[14]

In this case, cognitive theory helped investigators understand how Chinese intelligence was able to exploit Shriver's desires and aspirations for a career in government and international relations. Through psychological manipulation and flattery, Chinese intelligence officers convinced Shriver to apply for US government jobs with the intention of using his access to collect sensitive information.

Cognitive theory also helped investigators understand how Shriver rationalized his actions, as he believed that he was merely providing analysis and research to his Chinese contacts and did not consider himself a spy.

---

[14]For details, see Mattis, P. (2010). Shriver Case Highlights Traditional Chinese Espionage. *Jamestown Foundation China Brief, 10.*

Ultimately, Shriver was caught and jailed by US authorities. The use of cognitive theory allowed investigators to gain insight into the motivations and thought processes of the individual being recruited by a foreign intelligence agency, which helped them identify and prevent further damage to US national security.

Summary

The human factors involved in successful counterintelligence are magnified by the cyber environment.[15] The internet can make people vulnerable to influence operations or covert action including:

- *Social media*: Social media platforms can be used to target individuals with tailored messaging for misinformation and disinformation. This can make it more difficult for people to identify the truth and can make them more susceptible to manipulation.
- *Online communities*: Online communities work by building trust with individuals, allowing intelligence agents to manipulate and recruit those at risk.[16]
- *Phishing and malware*: Phishing can result in the compromise of an individual's computer or phone.[17] This can make them more vulnerable to intelligence gathering or manipulation.
- *Search Engine Optimization (SEO)*: Intelligence agencies can use SEO techniques to make sure that their propaganda or disinformation appears at the top of search engine results, making it more likely to be seen and believed by people.
- *Deepfake and AI generated videos*: Intelligence agencies can use deepfake and AI generated videos to manipulate people's perceptions of reality, spreading disinformation and propaganda.
- *Online gaming and virtual worlds*: Intelligence agencies can use online gaming and virtual worlds to establish relationships with individuals, making them more vulnerable to recruitment or manipulation.

In summary, the internet has made it easier for intelligence agencies to conduct influence operations and covert action, as it provides platforms that can be used to gather information, build relationships, and manipulate people.

---

[15] For a review, see Ceesay, E. N., Myers, K., & Watters, P. A. (2018). Human-centered strategies for cyber-physical systems security. *EAI Endorsed Transactions on Security and Safety*, 4(14).

[16] For an analysis, see Kelarev, A. V., Brown, S., Watters, P., Wu, X. W., & Dazeley, R. (2011). Establishing reasoning communities of security experts for internet commerce security. In *Technologies for Supporting Reasoning Communities and Collaborative Decision Making: Cooperative Approaches* (pp. 380–396). IGI Global.

[17] For an example, see Alazab, M., Venkatraman, S., Watters, P., & Alazab, M. (2013). Information security governance: the art of detecting hidden malware. In *IT security governance innovations: theory and research* (pp. 293–315). IGI Global.

Chapter 5
Counterespionage

Counterespionage refers to efforts to prevent or detect espionage activities conducted by foreign governments or other adversaries. The elements of counterespionage typically include:

- *Intelligence gathering*: Collecting information about potential espionage threats, such as the identities and activities of foreign intelligence agents and their methods of operation.
- *Security measures*: Implementing physical, personnel, and information security measures to protect against espionage activities. This can include background checks and security clearances.
- *Counterintelligence operations*: Conducting operations to identify and neutralize foreign intelligence agents, such as surveillance, counter surveillance, and the use of deception and disinformation.
- *Information analysis*: Analyzing information to identify patterns, trends, and potential threats related to espionage activities.
- *Interagency and international cooperation*: Coordinating with other agencies and foreign partners to share information and resources and to conduct joint operations.
- *Cybersecurity*: Implementing security measures and protocols to protect against cyber espionage and cyber attacks.
- *Employee training*: Educating employees and contractors on how to identify and report suspicious activities, and how to protect sensitive information.
- *Legal measures*: Having in place laws that criminalize espionage and support the investigation and prosecution of spies.
- *Publicity:* Highlighting the importance of protecting sensitive information.

One recent case study for successful counterespionage is the dismantling of a Russian spy network by European intelligence agencies in 2018. The spy network was reportedly run by the Russian intelligence agency, GRU, and involved several individuals across multiple countries who were recruited to spy for Russia.[1]

The operation began in 2016 when Czech intelligence services identified and expelled two Russian diplomats for conducting espionage activities. This led to a wider investigation involving intelligence agencies from multiple European countries, including Germany, Poland, and the Netherlands.

Several people were arrested and charged with espionage-related offenses, including in GermanyIn the Netherlands, four Russian intelligence officers were expelled for attempting to hack the OPCW (Organization for the Prohibition of Chemical Weapons).

The success of this counterespionage operation was attributed to a few factors, including close collaboration between European intelligence agencies, increased awareness and vigilance about Russian intelligence activities, and the use of advanced technical capabilities to detect and disrupt Russian espionage efforts. Additionally, the public disclosure of these actions by European governments sent a strong message to Russia and other potential adversaries about the consequences of engaging in espionage activities in Europe.

Counterespionage is a complex and multi-disciplinary effort that requires coordination and cooperation between different agencies and organizations, as well tactics procedures used by foreign intelligence services.

Intelligence Gathering

Intelligence gathering is increasingly reliant on cyber capabilities. Historically, the following methods used to gather intelligence for counterespionage:

- *Human intelligence (HUMINT)*: This type of intelligence is gathered using human sources, such as informants, defectors, and undercover agents. These sources can provide valuable information about the identities, activities, and methods of foreign intelligence agents.
- *Signals intelligence (SIGINT)*: This type of intelligence is gathered through the collection and analysis of electronic communications, such as radio transmissions, telephone conversations, and internet traffic. SIGINT can be used to identify the location and activities of foreign intelligence agents, as well as to gather information about their methods of communication and encryption.
- *Imagery intelligence (IMINT):* This type of intelligence is gathered using visual or photographic means, such as satellite imagery, aerial reconnaissance, and ground-based cameras. IMINT can track foreign intelligence agents, as well as to gather information about their operational capabilities.
- *Open-source intelligence (OSINT)*: Gathered from publicly available sources, such as newspapers, magazines, books, television, and the internet. OSINT can

---

[1] For details, see https://www.washingtonpost.com/world/europe/how-russias-military-intelligence-agency-became-the-covert-muscle-in-putins-duels-with-the-west/2018/12/27/2736bbe2-fb2d-11e8-8c9a-860ce2a8148f_story.html

be used to gather information about the political, economic, and social conditions in foreign countries, as well as to identify potential espionage threats.[2]

- *Cyber intelligence*: Derived from watching the digital activities and data from networks, devices, and cyber actors. Cyber intelligence can be used to identify potential cyber espionage threats as well as to gather information about the methods, tactics, and techniques of cyber adversaries.
- *Financial intelligence*: Examines financial transactions and data to uncover illicit activities such as money laundering, financing of criminal activities, and illicit funding for espionage.

One example of how HUMINT (human intelligence) has supported counterespionage since 2015 is the case of the former CIA officer Jerry Chun Shing Lee. Lee was arrested in 2018 and charged with conspiring to spy for China. According to the indictment, Lee met with Chinese intelligence officers in hotels in Hong Kong and Shenzhen and was paid for providing them with data about CIA activities in China.[3]

The case was built on a combination of electronic surveillance and human intelligence. In 2012, the CIA began noticing a pattern of communication between Chinese intelligence officers and their informants, which led them to suspect that there was a mole within their organization. They launched a massive internal investigation, which included reviewing travel records, interviewing hundreds of employees, and analyzing email and other electronic communications.

In the end, it was a combination of electronic surveillance and HUMINT that led to Lee's arrest. According to court documents, the FBI used surveillance cameras and other surveillance techniques to track Lee's movements, and enlisted the help of former CIA colleagues who knew Lee and were able to provide valuable insights into his character and behavior.

The case highlights the importance of HUMINT in counterespionage operations, particularly in cases involving insider threats. While electronic surveillance can provide valuable information, it is often HUMINT that allows investigators to put the pieces together and understand the motivations and actions of the individuals involved.

Using SIGINT

The key elements of SIGINT include:

- *Collection*: This involves the gathering of signals and communications through various means, such as electronic surveillance, interception, or monitoring.
- *Processing*: Once the signals and communications are collected, they need to be processed and transformed into a usable format for analysis. This involves tasks such as decryption, translation, and formatting.

---

[2] For an overview and some very detailed examples, see Layton, R., & Watters, P. A. (2015). *Automating open source intelligence: Algorithms for OSINT*. Syngress.

[3] For a summary, see Dorfman, Z. (2018). Botched CIA communications system helped blow cover of Chinese agents. *Foreign Policy, Aug.*

- *Analysis*: This involves examining the processed signals and communications to identify relevant information and intelligence. This can include identifying key individuals, locations, or activities, as well as determining patterns, trends, or threats.
- *Dissemination*: Once the intelligence is identified, it needs to be disseminated to relevant stakeholders, such as government agencies, military units, or law enforcement organizations, to support their missions and decision-making.
- *Protection*: Finally, SIGINT operations need to be protected from detection and disruption by hostile actors. This can involve employing various security measures, such as encryption, compartmentalization, and physical security.

One example of a case where signals intelligence (SIGINT) has been used for counterespionage is the Venona project. Venona was a top-secret U.S. Army intelligence program that ran from 1943 to 1980. The program was tasked with the decryption of Soviet diplomatic and intelligence communications that were intercepted by the US.[4]

The Venona project was able to decrypt and translate thousands of Soviet messages, providing valuable insights. The decrypted messages revealed the identities of several Soviet spies who had infiltrated the U.S. government, including the nuclear secrets. This information was used to identify and neutralize Soviet agents and to protect U.S. military and atomic secrets.

In another example, In the early 2010s, the NSA used SIGINT to uncover a Chinese cyber espionage campaign targeting U.S companies and government agencies. The Chinese government-sponsored hackers were using advanced malware and hacking techniques to steal sensitive information from U.S. targets. The NSA was able to identify the Chinese hackers' infrastructure, tactics, and tools through the collection and analysis of electronic communications. This information was shared with U.S. companies and government agencies to protect against future cyber espionage attacks.[5]

These examples demonstrate how SIGINT can be used to identify and neutralize espionage activities and to protect sensitive information. The use of SIGINT in counterespionage requires advanced technical capabilities and tactics and procedures used by foreign intelligence services.

Using OSINT

OSINT, or Open-Source Intelligence, refers to the collection, analysis, and dissemination of information from publicly available sources. The following are some of the key characteristics of OSINT:

---

[4] For a summary, see Frazier, P. (2010). The venona project and cold war espionage. *OAH Magazine of History*, *24*(4), 35–39.

[5] For details, see Gutmann, E. (2010). Hacker nation: China's cyber assault. *World Affs.*, *173*, 70.

- *Sources*: OSINT is derived from a wide range of sources, including news media, social media, blogs, public records, academic research, and other publicly available information.
- *Accessibility*: Unlike classified information, OSINT is publicly available and often only requires access to public records.
- *Volume*: The amount of available OSINT is massive and constantly growing, making it a valuable source of intelligence.
- *Analysis*: OSINT requires skilled analysts to sift through and make sense of the vast amount of information available.
- *Verification*: As OSINT is often sourced from non-experts and non-traditional sources, it requires careful verification to ensure accuracy and reliability.
- *Integration*: OSINT is often used in conjunction with other forms of intelligence, such as HUMINT, SIGINT, and GEOINT, to provide a comprehensive picture of a particular topic or situation.

One example of a case where open-source intelligence (OSINT) has been used to uncover a mole is Aldrich Ames, from 1994.[6]

The CIA had been investigating Ames for several years but was unable to gather enough evidence to prosecute him. However, in 1993, a team of CIA counterintelligence officers began to use OSINT techniques to gather information about Ames' activities and financial status. They discovered that Ames had been living beyond his means, despite his relatively modest salary. The officers also uncovered that Ames had purchased a house and a Jaguar car and was taking expensive vacations.

The CIA team then used this information to create a detailed financial profile of Ames, which they compared to the lifestyles of other CIA employees. The comparison revealed that Ames' financial situation was highly unusual and inconsistent with his salary. This information, combined with other evidence, was used to build a case against Ames and to uncover his espionage activities.

Another example, in 2010, Robert Philip Hanssen of the FBI was found to be spying for the Russian government. The investigation was led by the FBI's counterintelligence division, which used OSINT techniques to gather information about Hanssen's activities, including his financial records, phone records, and internet usage. The investigation revealed that Hanssen had been passing classified information to the Russians for more than 15 years, and that he had received more than $1.4 million in cash and diamonds in return.[7]

In both of these cases, OSINT techniques were used to gather information about the suspects' activities and financial status, which helped to uncover their espionage activities. These examples demonstrate how OSINT can be used to identify and neutralize espionage activities and to protect sensitive information.

---

[6] For details, see Carr, C. (1994). Aldrich Ames and the conduct of American intelligence. *World Policy Journal*, *11*(3), 19–28.

[7] For an outline, see Sanford, J. S., & Arrigo, B. A. (2007). Policing and psychopathy: The case of robert philip hanssen. *Journal of forensic psychology practice*, *7*(3), 1–31.

Using Cyber Intelligence

The characteristics of cyber intelligence include:

- *Technical expertise*: Cyber intelligence requires specialized technical knowledge of computer systems, networks, and security.
- *Timeliness*: The ability to collect and analyze information in real-time is critical in the rapidly evolving world of cyber threats.
- *Multidisciplinary approach*: Cyber intelligence requires a multidisciplinary approach, involving experts in technical, legal, and policy[8] fields.
- *Collaboration*: Effective cyber intelligence relies on collaboration between different organizations and agencies, including intelligence agencies, law enforcement, and private sector entities.
- *Threat assessment*: Cyber intelligence involves the assessment of potential threats, including state-sponsored attacks, criminal activity, and cyber terrorism.
- *Attribution*: Cyber intelligence seeks to identify the source of attacks, including the individuals, organizations, or states responsible for cyber threats.[9]
- *Risk management*: Cyber intelligence helps organizations and governments manage risk by identifying vulnerabilities and implementing measures to mitigate potential threats.
- *Continuous monitoring*: Cyber intelligence requires continuous monitoring of networks and systems to identify new threats and vulnerabilities.
- *Adaptability*: Cyber intelligence needs to be adaptable to evolving threats and changing technologies, as cybercriminals and other threat actors are constantly developing new tactics and techniques.

Cyber intelligence has been used to identify false flags, which are covert operations designed to deceive or mislead. In cyber operations, false flags are often used to conceal the identity of the attacker.

One example of a case where cyber intelligence was used to identify a false flag is the Operation Aurora incident in 2010.[10] Operation Aurora was a cyber espionage campaign that targeted several major U.S. companies and government agencies, including Google, Adobe, and RSA. The attackers were able to steal sensitive information and intellectual property from the companies.

---

[8] For a policy review, see Kayes, A. S. M., Hammoudeh, M., Badsha, S., Watters, P. A., Ng, A., Mohammed, F., & Islam, M. (2020). Responsibility Attribution Against Data Breaches. In *2020 IEEE International Conference on Informatics, IoT, and Enabling Technologies (ICIoT)* (pp. 498–503). IEEE.

[9] For an example, see Layton, R., Perez, C., Birregah, B., Watters, P., & Lemercier, M. (2013). Indirect information linkage for OSINT through authorship analysis of aliases. In *Trends and Applications in Knowledge Discovery and Data Mining: PAKDD 2013 International Workshops: DMApps, DANTH, QIMIE, BDM, CDA, CloudSD, Gold Coast, QLD, Australia, April 14–17, 2013, Revised Selected Papers 17* (pp. 36–46). Springer Berlin Heidelberg.

[10] For a review, see Xirasagar, S., & Mojtahed, M. (2010). Featured this month. *Network Security*.

At first, the Chinese government was blamed for the attacks, but further investigation revealed that the attackers were based in Russia. The attackers had used several techniques to conceal their tracks, using malware that was designed to evade detection.

The investigation team used several cyber intelligence techniques, such as forensic analysis, network traffic analysis, and malware reverse engineering to identify the true origin of the attack. They were able to identify hosts which were located in Russia.

Another example is the case of the NotPetya malware attack in 2017. The malware was at first thought to be a variant of the Petya malware, which was known for encrypting victims' data and demanding a ransom. But further investigations revealed that the malware was a wiper malware, designed to destroy the data of the victims, and was used in a false flag operation. The Ukrainian government and several security researchers found that the attackers had used Ukrainian-language resources and infrastructure to make the attack look like it was launched by Ukrainian hackers. The investigation team used OSINT and forensic analysis to reveal that the malware was developed by Russian state-sponsored hackers.[11]

These examples demonstrate how cyber intelligence can be used to identify false flags by using different techniques like forensic analysis, network traffic analysis, malware reverse engineering, and OSINT. These techniques help to uncover the true origin of an attack and to reveal the identity of the attackers, which can be used to protect against future attacks.

Using Imagery Intelligence

IMINT can support counterintelligence by providing visual information that can help to identify and disrupt foreign intelligence activities. Some ways that IMINT can support counterintelligence include:

- *Surveillance and Monitoring*: IMINT can be used to monitor the activities of foreign intelligence agencies, including the deployment of agents, the establishment of spy networks, and the transportation of sensitive materials. This information can help to identify potential threats and support counterintelligence efforts.
- *Target Analysis*: IMINT can be used to analyze and assess potential targets, including military installations, government facilities, and other key assets. This information can help to identify vulnerabilities and support counterintelligence efforts to protect these assets.
- *Threat Assessment*: IMINT can be used to assess potential threats, including the presence of extremist groups, and the potential for hostile activities. This

---

[11] For a great outline, see Greenberg, A. (2018). The untold story of NotPetya, the most devastating cyberattack in history. *Wired, August*, 22.

information can help to inform counterintelligence efforts to prevent or disrupt these threats.

- *Evidence Collection*: IMINT can be used to collect evidence to support investigations into foreign intelligence activities. This may include the collection of images and video footage of individuals or activities that may be of interest to counterintelligence agencies.
- *Situational Awareness*: IMINT can support counterintelligence operations through real-time monitoring. This may include the ability to monitor the movements of individuals or groups, to track the deployment of resources, or to monitor changes in the operational environment.

By using IMINT to support counterintelligence, governments and intelligence agencies can gain a better understanding of foreign intelligence activities and take steps to disrupt them. However, it is significant to note that IMINT is just one tool in the arsenal of counterintelligence, and that a comprehensive and multi-disciplinary approach is required to effectively address this threat.

Pulling it all together, Operation Ghost Stories provides an example of how a range of intelligence gathering approaches can be used to support counterespionage. In the mid-2000s, the US Federal Bureau of Investigation (FBI) conducted a major counterintelligence operation against the Russian Foreign Intelligence Service (SVR).[12] "Operation Ghost Stories" aimed to disrupt and dismantle the SVR's spy network in the United States.

The FBI used OSINT as a key tool in the operation. They collected and analyzed vast amounts of open-source information, including social media profiles, online forums, and other public sources of information. This allowed them to identify individuals who were connected to the SVR and to monitor their activities and communications.

By using OSINT, the FBI was able to gather critical information about the SVR's spy network, including their operational methods, targets, and locations. This information helped the FBI to identify key members of the spy network, to monitor their movements, and to intercept their communications.

In 2010, the FBI arrested ten individuals who were part of the SVR spy network in the United States. These individuals had been living in the US under deep cover, posing as ordinary citizens while they conducted espionage activities on behalf of the SVR. The arrests marked a major victory for the FBI, as it disrupted the SVR's spy network and prevented the Russians from gathering sensitive information about US national security.

The Operation Ghost Stories case study demonstrates the value of OSINT in counterintelligence. By using OSINT to gather and analyze vast amounts of open-source information, the FBI was able to identify and disrupt a major espionage threat to US national security. The operation also highlights the importance of using

---

[12] For analysis, see Riehle, K. P. (2021). The ghosts of Russian intelligence: the challenges and evolution of Russia's illegals program. *Intelligence and National Security*, *36*(6), 918–924.

a multi-disciplinary approach to counterintelligence, as OSINT was used in conjunction with other intelligence disciplines, such as SIGINT and IMINT, to support the FBI's efforts.

Summary

A wide range of intelligence gathering approaches can be used to support a counterintelligence program. The precise scale, scope and mix of approaches will be determined by the specific use cases, operational requirements, and – most significantly – budget.

Chapter 6
Technical Surveillance

Technical surveillance means using technology to gather data for intelligence activities. Technical surveillance can be used to support counterintelligence in several ways:

- *Monitoring Communications*: Technical surveillance can be used to monitor the communications of people engaging in spying or other intelligence activities. This can include intercepting telephone calls, monitoring email and social media accounts, or tracking the movements of individuals through GPS or other location-based technologies.
- *Technical Countermeasures*: Technical surveillance can also be used to detect and disrupt technical countermeasures used by espionage or intelligence organizations. This can include monitoring the use of encryption technologies, detecting the use of spy satellites or other remote-sensing technologies, or using signal-jamming technology to disrupt communications.
- *Physical Surveillance*: Technical surveillance can also be used to support physical surveillance operations. For example, cameras, microphones, and other sensors can be placed in strategic locations to monitor the movements and activities of suspected individuals or organizations. Physical Surveillance is covered in Chap. 7.
- *Data Analysis*: Technical surveillance can also suggest the presence of intelligence activities. This can include using data analytics tools to identify correlations between individuals or organizations or using machine learning algorithms to detect suspicious behavior. Data Analysis is further described in Chap. 8.

One example of Technical Countermeasures being used for counterespionage in the cyber age is the case of the Chinese hacking group known as APT10. In December 2018, it was reported that the US Department of Justice had indicted two members of the group, Zhu Hua and Zhang Shilong, for their involvement in a hacking campaign that targeted a range of industries, including aviation, satellite technology, and pharmaceuticals.[1]

As part of the investigation, Technical Countermeasures were used to detect and monitor the group's activities. The US government and private cybersecurity firms reportedly deployed advanced threat detection tools to detect the group's presence on targeted networks, and then used advanced forensics to trace the group's activities back to its original source.

According to the indictment, APT10 stole sensitive information from multiple organizations, including technological data. The use of Technical Countermeasures helped to identify and track the group's activities, which ultimately led to the indictment of two of its members.

This case demonstrates the importance of Technical Countermeasures in countering cyber espionage, particularly in identifying and detecting the presence of sophisticated hacking groups. The use of advanced threat detection and forensic tools may assist organizations and can play a critical role in supporting counterintelligence efforts.

By using technical surveillance to gather and analyze information, counterintelligence organizations can gain a better understanding of threats from espionage and associated activities and take appropriate measures to disrupt these activities and protect national security. Technical surveillance can be used in conjunction with other intelligence disciplines, such as HUMINT, OSINT, and SIGINT, to support a multi-disciplinary approach to counterintelligence. In this chapter, the focus is on communications monitoring and technical countermeasures as examples of both the challenges and opportunities facing counterintelligence.

Communications Monitoring

There are several ways in which communications can be monitored:

- *Wiretapping*: This involves intercepting the signals of a communication, such as a telephone call or an internet connection, and listening to the content of the communication.
- *Email and Social Media Monitoring*: This involves monitoring the content of emails and social media accounts for specific keywords or phrases that may indicate suspicious activity.
- *Location Tracking*: This involves tracking the location of a person or device through GPS or other location-based technologies, even cookies[2]!

---

[1] For a review, see Manantan, M. (2019). Cyber dimension of the South China Sea clashes. *The Diplomat*, 5.

[2] For a case study, see Shuford, E., Kavanaugh, T., Ralph, B., Ceesay, E., & Watters, P. (2018). Measuring personal privacy breaches using third-party trackers. In *2018 17th IEEE International Conference on Trust, Security and Privacy in Computing and Communications/12th IEEE*

- *Deep Packet Inspection (DPI)*: This involves examining the contents of data packets transmitted over a network, such as the internet, to identify and analyze their contents.
- *Mobile Device Monitoring*: This involves monitoring the activities of cell devices or tablets, to gather information about the user's activities and movements.
- *Interception of Radio Signals*: This involves intercepting the signals of radio communications, such as those used by law enforcement or military organizations, to gather information about their activities.
- *Voice Recognition*: This involves using voice recognition technology to identify the speaker of a communication, such as a telephone call or voice recording.

These methods of monitoring communications can be used individually or in combination to gather information for intelligence purposes. However, it is significant to note that many of these methods may be subject to legal restrictions and may require a warrant or other legal authority to be used.

One example of Deep Packet Inspection (DPI) being used to support counterintelligence is the case of the Syrian Electronic Army (SEA) in 2014. The SEA hacking group used various methods to infiltrate and disrupt the online operations of its targets, including media organizations and government agencies.[3]

In response, the U.S. government used DPI to monitor and block the SEA's communications, allowing them to identify the group's tactics, techniques, and procedures (TTPs), as well as their command-and-control infrastructure. This information was then used to launch targeted cyber operations against the SEA, disrupting their activities and reducing their effectiveness.

DPI was a crucial component of this operation, as it allowed the U.S. government to inspect and analyze the content of the SEA's network traffic in real time. This enabled them to identify and block malicious traffic, as well as to extract valuable intelligence about the group's capabilities and intentions.

Examining the approaches used in more detail, starting with DPI. It is a technique used to examine the contents of data packets transmitted over a network, such as the internet, in real-time. The process works as follows:

- *Data Packet Capture*: Data packets are captured as they pass through a network, typically at a network gateway or switch.
- *Packet Decoding*: The captured data packets are decoded to reveal their contents, including the source and destination addresses, packet type, and payload.
- *Content Inspection*: The payload of the data packet is inspected to determine its contents, such as emails, instant messages, web pages, or other types of data.

International Conference on Big Data Science and Engineering (TrustCom/BigDataSE) (pp. 1615–1618). IEEE.

[3] For a case study, see Dávila A, S., Guruli, N., & Samaro, D. (2021). DIGITAL DOMINION: How the Syrian regime's mass digital surveillance violates human rights.

- *Signature Matching*: The contents of the data packet are compared against a database of known signatures, such as malware or other types of malicious code, to determine if the packet contains any malicious content.[4]
- *Response*: Based on the results of the inspection, the DPI system may take action to block the data packet, allow it to pass through the network, or take some other action, such as logging the packet for further analysis.

A worked example of DPI could be as follows:

- A user attempts to access a website that is known to host malicious content.
- The data packets associated with the website request are captured by the DPI system.
- The payload of the data packets is decoded and inspected to determine its contents.
- The contents of the data packets are compared against a database of known signatures, and the system determines that the website contains malicious code.
- The DPI system blocks the data packets associated with the website request, preventing the user from accessing the malicious content.

For counterespionage purposes, DPI can be used to support counterintelligence efforts by providing visibility into the contents of data packets transmitted over a network, such as the internet. By examining the contents of data packets, DPI can help identify and prevent the exfiltration of sensitive information, as well as detect attempts to infiltrate a network.

A worked example of how DPI can be used for counterespionage is as follows:

- A foreign intelligence agency attempts to exfiltrate sensitive information from a government network.
- The DPI system captures the data packets associated with the exfiltration attempt.
- The payload of the data packets is decoded and inspected to determine its contents.
- The contents of the data packets are compared against a database of known signatures, and the system determines that the data contains sensitive information.
- The DPI system blocks the data packets associated with the exfiltration attempt, preventing the foreign intelligence agency from accessing the sensitive information.
- The DPI system logs the details of the exfiltration attempt, including the source and destination addresses, the type of data being exfiltrated, and any other relevant information.

By using DPI to monitor network traffic and detect attempts to exfiltrate sensitive information, organizations can improve their ability to defend against counterespionage efforts and protect their valuable information assets.

---

[4] For a more abstract approach, see Kelarev, A., Yearwood, J., & Watters, P. (2010). Internet security applications of Gröbner-Shirshov bases. *Asian-European Journal of Mathematics*, *3*(03), 435–442.

While DPI works well with plaintext analysis, unfortunately, the large-scale presence of encryption in internet protocols has restricted its use in recent years. DPI can face several challenges in the presence of encryption, including:

- *Encryption Bypass*: Encryption can be used to bypass DPI systems, as encrypted data packets are not easily inspectable. This can make it difficult for DPI systems to determine the contents of encrypted data packets and take appropriate action.
- *Performance Overhead*: Decrypting and re-encrypting encrypted data packets can place a significant performance overhead on DPI systems, potentially affecting network performance.
- *Key Management*: Managing encryption keys can be hard in large, complex networks. DPI systems must be able to securely manage encryption keys to effectively inspect encrypted data packets.
- *Privacy Concerns*: The use of DPI to inspect encrypted data packets can raise privacy concerns, as it requires organizations to access and potentially store sensitive data.
- *Interoperability*: DPI systems may not be able to inspect encrypted data packets if they are not interoperable with the encryption technology being used.

These challenges highlight the importance of selecting DPI systems that are capable of handling encrypted data, as well as considering the impact of encryption on In summary network security when deploying encryption technologies. Organizations should also consider implementing encryption best practices, such as using strong encryption algorithms and regularly rotating encryption keys, to minimize the risk of encryption bypass.

An alternative to DPI is to use malware to compromise network endpoints, thereby bypassing the need to inspect and analyze the plaintext of packets. This can be done by infecting endpoints with malware that allows attackers to intercept and exfiltrate encrypted data before it is encrypted or after it is decrypted.

For example, an attacker might use a remote access Trojan (RAT) to infect an endpoint and gain access to sensitive information before it is encrypted. The attacker can then exfiltrate the sensitive information in an unencrypted form, bypassing the encryption protections provided by DPI systems. RATs typically work by establishing a persistent connection between the attacker and the infected endpoint, allowing the attacker to execute commands, exfiltrate data, and perform other malicious activities.[5]

One well-known RAT is called Poison Ivy. Poison Ivy is a RAT that is often used to steal personal data. It works through establishing a persistent presence on the endpoint.[6]

---

[5] For an example, see Lobo, D., Watters, P., Wu, X. W., & Sun, L. (2010, July). Windows rootkits: Attacks and countermeasures. In *2010 Second Cybercrime and Trustworthy Computing Workshop* (pp. 69–78). IEEE.

[6] For an outline, see Bennett, J. T., Moran, N., & Villeneuve, N. (2013). Poison ivy: Assessing damage and extracting intelligence. *FireEye Threat Research Blog*.

To infect a target, Poison Ivy is typically delivered to the target via a phishing email, social engineering attack, or through the exploitation of a vulnerability in the target's system. Once installed, Poison Ivy establishes a covert connection with the attacker's C2 server, which can be used to execute commands and exfiltrate data.

Poison Ivy is considered one of the more advanced RATs, as it uses encryption and other techniques to evade detection and persist on infected systems. As a result, organizations must be proactive in implementing endpoint security measures, such as anti-malware software and firewalls, to minimize the risk of infection.

In addition, attackers may use malware to perform man-in-the-middle (MITM) attacks, intercepting encrypted data as it is transmitted between endpoints and modifying or exfiltrating the data before it is encrypted or after it is decrypted. For example, consider a scenario where two governments are communicating sensitive information about a potential threat via encrypted email. An attacker could use a MITM attack to intercept the email communication between the two governments, modify the content of the email, and exfiltrate the sensitive information to a third party.

To do this, the hacker would need to position themselves between the two communicating parties and intercept the encrypted email communication. They would then use tools to modify the content of the email and exfiltrate the sensitive information to a third party.

MITM attacks can be difficult to detect and prevent, as the attacker is positioned between the two communicating parties and is able to intercept and modify encrypted communications. To minimize the risk of MITM attacks, organizations should implement strong encryption technologies, such as SSL/TLS, and regularly update their systems to ensure that vulnerabilities are patched. They should also educate users about safe computing practices, such as verifying the authenticity of SSL certificates, to help prevent MITM attacks.

SSL certificates can be verified to ensure that the certificate is valid, and that the website is indeed what it claims to be. Described below are some common ways to verify SSL certificates:

- *Check the SSL Certificate Information*: When a secure connection is established, the SSL certificate information can be viewed by clicking on the padlock icon in the address bar. This information includes the certificate and domain name that the certificate was issued to.
- *Verify the Certificate Authority (CA)*: The CA that issued the certificate can be verified by checking if it is listed in the trusted root CA store of the browser or operating system. Browsers typically come pre-configured with a list of trusted root CAs.
- *Check the Certificate Chain*: The certificate chain is a series of digital certificates that link the website's certificate to a trusted root CA. The certificate chain can be viewed in the SSL certificate information and should be checked to ensure that it is complete and that each certificate in the chain is valid.

- *Verify the SSL Certificate Expiration Date*: The SSL certificate should be checked to ensure that it has not expired. An expired certificate can indicate that the website is no longer secure and that the certificate has not been updated.
- *Check the SSL Seal*: Some websites display an SSL seal to indicate that they use SSL encryption, and that the SSL certificate has been verified by a trusted CA. These seals can be clicked on to view the certificate information and verify its validity.

By verifying SSL certificates, connecting to a valid website is easy, and people can be assured that their sensitive information, such as login credentials and financial information, is being transmitted securely. However, the astute reader will realise that the "trust" placed in many of these entities may be misguided, and that the secure communications process can be compromised in several ways.

One example of a root CA compromise is the DigiNotar incident in 2011 – this certificate authority compromised by an attacker who used the access to issue fraudulent digital certificates for several high-profile websites, including Google, Mozilla, and Skype.[7]

The attacker was able to issue these fraudulent certificates because DigiNotar was a trusted root CA, and the digital certificates were trusted by browsers and operating systems. This allowed the attacker to intercept and decrypt encrypted communications between users and the targeted websites, effectively allowing the attacker to potentially gather a range of commercial and personal data.

As a result of the compromise, major browsers, including Google Chrome and Mozilla Firefox, removed DigiNotar from their list of trusted root CAs. DigiNotar went bankrupt shortly thereafter.

This incident serves as a reminder that even trusted root CAs can be compromised, and it is important to continuously monitor and assess the security posture of root CAs to ensure that they maintain their trusted status. It also highlights the importance of using encryption and secure certificate issuance processes to prevent attackers from obtaining false certificates and compromising the trust in digital certificates.

Technical Countermeasures

The main countermeasures to technical surveillance are:

- *Encryption*: Using encryption to prevent plaintext data from being read.
- *Authentication*: making sure that only the right individuals have access to sensitive information.

---

[7] For details, see Prins, J. R., & Cybercrime, B. U. (2011). Diginotar certificate authority breach "operation black tulip". *Fox-IT, November, 18*.

- *Physical security*: Protecting the physical location of sensitive information and communications devices by implementing access controls, monitoring, and alarm systems.
- *Software security*: Keeping software up to date and applying patches to fix known vulnerabilities, as well as remediating weaknesses in software systems.
- *Network security*: The standard range of measures typically suggested by a blue team.
- *Training*: Making sure that staff don't do the wrong things (most of the time).
- *Third-party security*: Assessing and monitoring the security posture of third-party vendors, such as cloud service providers, to ensure that they are following best practices and meeting security requirements.

Encryption, as described above, is vulnerable to compromise as described above. Authentication systems are highly vulnerable to compromise, including:

- *Weak Passwords*: One of the most common and easily preventable issues with authentication systems is weak or easily guessable passwords
- *Credential Stuffing*: This attack involves using lists of stolen login credentials to automate login attempts on a targeted system
- *Session Hijacking*: Session hijacking refers to an attacker intercepting and taking over an active user session, usually by stealing a session token or cookie. Worse still, most encryption systems depend on strong authentication! Thus, designing and implementing systems that avoid these weaknesses, is an essential counter-measure – including biometrics.

Even widely used and standardized cryptosystems are susceptible to attacks on their underlying mathematics. The Advanced Encryption Standard (AES) is a common encryption algorithm that is considered secure and difficult to crack. However, in 2011, a team of researchers led by Josef Pieprzyk announced that they had discovered a way to crack the AES encryption using a technique known as the biclique attack.

The biclique attack involves building a graph of the AES cipher and then searching for patterns in the graph that can be exploited to recover the key. This attack requires an enormous amount of computational power and memory, but the researchers were able to demonstrate that it was possible to recover a 128-bit AES key using a relatively modest cluster of computers.[8]

Pieprzyk's team's work was significant because it demonstrated that even highly secure encryption algorithms like AES can be vulnerable to attack under certain conditions. This has led to further research into more secure encryption techniques and the development of new countermeasures to protect against attacks like the biclique attack.

Physical access to cyber-physical systems, such as through theft or unauthorized access to control rooms, can lead to significant consequences such as theft of sensitive information or disruption of critical systems. Improving physical security

---

[8] For an account, see https://www.science.org/content/article/crucial-cipher-questioned

should therefore be a priority for breach prevention. Specific areas of concern include:

1. *Unsecured Entry Points*: Unsecured or easily accessible doors, windows, and vents can be a major vulnerability for physical security.
2. *Insufficient Surveillance*: A lack of surveillance cameras or inadequate monitoring can make it easier for unauthorized individuals to access a secure facility.
3. *Poor Access Control*: Weaknesses in access control, such as easily bypassed locks or unsecured access cards, can make it easier for unauthorized individuals to gain entry to a secure area.
4. *Human Error*: Human error, such as leaving doors unlocked or giving out access credentials to unauthorized individuals, can also be a major vulnerability in physical security.
5. *Natural Disasters*: Natural disasters such as earthquakes, fires, and floods can disrupt physical security systems and cause damage to secure facilities.

One noteworthy case where exploited human error contributed to counterintelligence was the 2013 cyber-attack on the US Navy's largest unclassified computer network, the Navy Marine Corps Intranet (NMCI).[9]

In this attack, Chinese hackers exploited the human error of a NMCI contractor who fell for a spear-phishing email. The malware allowed the hackers to gain access to the contractor's NMCI account and infiltrate the network.

Once inside the NMCI network, the hackers were able to access sensitive information, including emails, task lists, and other documents related to ongoing naval operations. The attack was only discovered when a cybersecurity firm that the Navy had hired to conduct a routine check found evidence of the intrusion.

The attack demonstrated the importance of employee training and awareness in preventing cyber-attacks. Had the contractor been trained to recognize and avoid spear-phishing emails, the attack could have been prevented. It also highlighted the need for organizations to regularly conduct testing to see if there are known vulnerabilities.

Securing software can prevent surveillance. The major strategies for software security include:

1. *Code Review and Testing*: Regularly reviewing and testing code is one of the most effective ways to identify and fix vulnerabilities in software.
2. *Security by Design*: Adopting a security-by-design approach, which involves incorporating security considerations into the software development process, can help prevent vulnerabilities from being introduced in the first place.
3. *Vulnerability Management*: Patching vulnerabilities in a timely manner can help reduce the risk of exploitation.
4. *Access Control*: Implementing strict access control measures and monitoring access to sensitive information can help prevent unauthorized access.

---

[9] For details, see Villeneuve, N., Moran, N., Haq, T., & Scott, M. (2013). Operation saffron rose. *FireEye Special Report*.

5. *Threat Intelligence*: Staying informed about emerging threats and incorporating threat intelligence into your security strategy can help you proactively defend against new and evolving threats.

One case study in Australia that illustrates how threat intelligence has supported counterintelligence is the Operation Byzantine Hades. In 2013, the Australian Signals Directorate (ASD) uncovered a cyber-espionage campaign that targeted various Australian government agencies, businesses, and universities. The campaign, which is believed to have originated in China, involved the use of a sophisticated piece of malware called "NetTraveler."

Using threat intelligence, the ASD was able to identify and track the activities of the hackers. The agency analyzed the malware used in the attack and identified its command-and-control infrastructure, which was in China. By analyzing the traffic to and from the command-and-control servers, the ASD was able to identify specific targets and track the activities of the hackers.[10]

The ASD shared its findings with the targeted organizations and others. The information provided by the ASD helped to improve the cybersecurity of the targeted organizations and allowed them to take steps to protect their sensitive information.

The use of threat intelligence in Operation Byzantine Hades demonstrates how intelligence agencies can use advanced technologies and analysis techniques to detect and prevent cyber-espionage activities. By collecting and analyzing data from various sources, such as network traffic, malware analysis, and social media, intelligence agencies can identify potential threats and provide warning and guidance to their constituents.

Network security can be similarly enhanced as a countermeasure. Above and beyond encryption and access control, discussed above, other strategies include Firewall Configuration, Network Segmentation and Regular Software Patching; and Monitoring and Detection: Implementing monitoring and detection systems, including through a Security Operations Centre (SOC).

Training across the board can also be an effective countermeasure. Some specific examples include:

1. *Awareness Training*: Raising awareness of security threats and best practices through education and training is one of the most effective techniques for improving cyber security.
2. *Hands-On Training*: Providing hands-on training and simulations makes people better prepared.
3. *Phishing Simulation*: Conducting phishing simulations can help employees learn to recognize and avoid phishing attempts.

---

[10] For an outline, see Taylor, P. J., Dargahi, T., & Dehghantanha, A. (2019). Analysis of apt actors targeting IoT and big data systems: Shell_crew, nettraveler, projectsauron, copykittens, volatile cedar and transparent tribe as a case study. *Handbook of big data and iot security*, 257–272.

4. *Role-Based Training*: Providing role-based training tailored to specific job responsibilities can help ensure that employees understand the specific security risks and requirements associated with their roles.
5. *Regular Refresher Training*: Regularly refreshing security training assists in maintaining their vigilance and effectiveness in protecting against cyber threats.
6. *Real-Life Scenario Training*: Training employees on real-life scenarios and case studies can help them understand the implications of security breaches and develop the critical thinking skills they need to respond effectively to security incidents.

Puling it all together, breach and attack simulations (BASs) are a security testing method that involves simulating real-world cyber-attacks and data breaches to evaluate controls and incident response processes. The goal of this type of simulation is to identify vulnerabilities and weaknesses in the security infrastructure, as well as to provide an opportunity for organizations to practice and improve their incident response capabilities.

There have been instances where BAS tools and techniques have been used by various organizations and agencies to identify vulnerabilities and test their cyber defenses against real-world cyber-attacks.

For example, in 2019, the French Ministry of Defense announced that it had launched a new cyber defense unit that would focus on strengthening the country's cyber defenses. The unit used a range of advanced tools and techniques, including breach and attack simulation, to identify vulnerabilities in the Ministry's network and systems. By simulating various types of attacks, the unit was able to identify weaknesses in its cyber defenses and take steps to address them.

Similarly, in 2020, the National Cyber Security Centre (NCSC) in the UK announced that it had launched a new program to help organizations improve their cyber defenses using BAS. The program, called Exercise in a Box,[11] provides organizations with a set of simulated cyber-attack scenarios that information training and awareness.

While these examples do not specifically relate to counterintelligence operations, they demonstrate how BAS can be used to identify vulnerabilities and improve cyber defenses, which can ultimately contribute to counterintelligence efforts by protecting against cyber threats and attacks.

This type of testing can include a variety of scenarios, such as simulated phishing attacks, network penetration tests, and simulated data breaches, to name a few. The results of the simulation can be used to improve security strategies and processes, as well as to provide employees with hands-on experience responding to security incidents. Attack and breach simulation is a valuable tool for organizations seeking to proactively improve their cyber security posture.

---

[11] Absolutely recommended! For details, see https://www.ncsc.gov.uk/information/exercise-in-a-box

Summary

Technical surveillance really lies at the heart of counterintelligence. A surveillance strategy can be devised to provide organizations with support, but also to implement appropriate countermeasures to neutralize potential threats. By proactively identifying and addressing potential security threats, organizations can minimize the risk of unauthorized surveillance and protect sensitive information and assets. In some cases, organizations must defend against threats, as well as undertaking their own surveillance.

Chapter 7
Physical Surveillance

Physical surveillance plays an important role in counterintelligence and counterespionage efforts. By monitoring and observing an organization's physical surroundings, it is possible to neutralize concerns such as foreign intelligence agents or business competitors who may be attempting to gather sensitive information. Physical surveillance can also help organizations identify and address security weaknesses in their facilities, such as unsecured access points, that could be exploited by adversaries.

Physical surveillance can take many forms, but in the cyber age, tend to focus on:

1. *Video and audio surveillance*: Video cameras and audio devices can be used to monitor access points, perimeter areas, and other critical locations, providing real-time or recorded footage that can be used to identify security incidents. These devices can also be remotely accessed through the internet!
2. *Web Surveillance*: Broadly speaking, typically using OSINT to monitor and track activity across the surface web, dark web and the physical world, often to place targets at both a potential crime scene, as well as being sources of intelligence.

Physical surveillance is typically used in conjunction with other counterintelligence and counterespionage techniques, such as technical surveillance countermeasures (Chap. 6) and information security measures, to provide a comprehensive and layered approach to security. By using physical surveillance to help identify and mitigate security threats, organizations can enhance their security posture and assets.

71
P. A. Watters, *Counterintelligence in a Cyber World*,
https://doi.org/10.1007/978-3-031-35287-4_7

Video

Video surveillance can be used for counterintelligence in several ways:

1. *Monitoring access points*: Video cameras can be used to monitor access points, such as doors, windows, and gates, to detect potential security breaches or unauthorized entry into secure areas.
2. *Observing perimeter areas*: Video cameras can be positioned around the perimeter of a facility to monitor for suspicious activity or potential security threats.
3. *Detecting suspicious behavior*: Video footage can be used to detect and track individuals who may be engaged in suspicious or hostile activity, such as surveillance or reconnaissance efforts.
4. *Identifying individuals*: Video cameras can capture images of individuals who may be involved in hostile or unauthorized activity, providing visual evidence that can be used to identify and track suspects.
5. *Verifying information*: Video footage can be used to verify information gathered from other sources, such as intelligence reports or eyewitness accounts, increasing reliability.

Video surveillance is a valuable tool for counterintelligence and can help organizations perceive and react to security concerns. By using video cameras to monitor their physical surroundings and to capture images of potential targets.

One well-known case study where video surveillance was used to obtain a conviction is the Boston Marathon bombing in 2013,[1] involving the two Tsarnaev brothers. After the bombing, the FBI and other law enforcement agencies used a vast network of video surveillance cameras in the area to identify the suspects. The cameras captured footage of the two brothers walking near the site of the bombings before and after the attack.

The FBI released the images and videos to the public, asking for help in identifying the suspects. The footage quickly spread across the media and social media, leading to a massive manhunt for the two brothers.

Eventually, one brother died, while the other was captured alive and later convicted of the bombings. The video surveillance footage played a critical role in identifying the suspects and ultimately obtaining a conviction in the case.

There are several video searching tools online that could be used for surveillance, including:

1. *Video management software (VMS)*: VMS is designed to capture, store, and manage video footage from surveillance cameras. Many VMS systems offer features such as real-time monitoring, remote access, and search capabilities that can be used to locate and review specific footage.

---

[1] For details, see Starbird, K., Maddock, J., Orand, M., Achterman, P., & Mason, R. M. (2014). Rumors, false flags, and digital vigilantes: Misinformation on twitter after the 2013 boston marathon bombing. *IConference 2014 proceedings*.

2. *Video analytics software*: Video analytics software can be used to analyze video footage and identify specific events or activities, such as movements of individuals or vehicles. This software can be used to search for and highlight specific incidents in a large amount of video footage.
3. *Face recognition technology*: Analyzes video footage to identify and track specific individuals using databases.[2]
4. *Object recognition technology*: Object recognition technology follows specific objects in footage, such as vehicles or packages. This technology can be used to search for and highlight specific objects in a large amount of video footage.
5. *Search engines*: Search engines, such as Google, can be used to search for publicly available video footage on the internet. This can be useful for identifying and locating video footage related to specific events or individuals.

These video searching tools can be used to quickly and efficiently search large amounts of video footage for specific incidents, individuals, or objects. There are numerous case studies – often portrayed in the negative – of how large-scale video surveillance can be misused.

Large-scale video surveillance in the United States has been misused in several ways, including:

- *Invasion of privacy*: Video surveillance cameras have been installed in public places like parks, sidewalks, and shopping malls. However, the indiscriminate use of cameras can lead to the invasion of privacy of innocent citizens.
- *Racial profiling*: There have been instances where video surveillance cameras have been used to target specific communities, particularly minority groups. This has led to accusations of racial profiling and discrimination.
- *Abuse of power*: Video surveillance footage can be misused by law enforcement agencies to target individuals or groups that are perceived as a threat, even if they have not committed any crimes. This can result in the abuse of power by law enforcement officials.
- *Inaccurate identification*: Video surveillance footage is not always clear, and the technology used to identify individuals can be inaccurate. This has led to instances where innocent people have been falsely accused or convicted of crimes based on faulty video surveillance evidence.
- *Lack of transparency*: The use of video surveillance cameras is often shrouded in secrecy, and there is a lack of transparency regarding how the footage is collected, stored, and analyzed. This has raised concerns about the potential for abuse and violations of civil liberties.

For the purposes of balance, large scale facial recognition software is widely used in China for a variety of purposes, including:

---

[2] Controversial! Even when you are buying bread and milk? For a case study, see https://ia.acs.org.au/article/2022/woolworths-expanding-surveillance-of-customers.html

1. *Public security*: The Chinese government uses facial recognition technology for public security purposes, such as tracking and identifying criminal suspects and monitoring public gatherings.
2. *Surveillance*: Facial recognition cameras are used in cities and public spaces to monitor the activities of citizens and collect data on their movements.
3. *Identity verification*: Facial recognition technology is used to verify the identity of individuals when accessing government services, banking services, and other sensitive information.
4. *Social monitoring*: Keeping track of the activities of a range of groups.
5. *Marketing and advertising*: Private companies use facial recognition technology for targeted marketing and advertising, using data collected from cameras to deliver targeted advertisements to individuals based on their demographics and behavior.

This widespread utilization of such systems naturally raises questions about equity, as well as the accuracy and fairness of the technology.[3] Facial recognition cameras usage and related technologies can also raise concerns about application of the technology for social control and censorship purposes.[4] Despite these concerns, governments continue to invest in and expand the use of facial recognition technology, positioning themselves as global leaders in the field.

Such systems are used in China for a wide range of applications, including surveillance, security, and convenience.[5] Described below are some examples:

- *Surveillance*: Used to monitor citizens, both in public spaces and online. This includes using facial recognition to identify and track potential criminals or political dissidents.
- *Security*: Facial recognition technology is also used in China to increase security in various settings, such as airports, train stations, and banks. For example, some Chinese banks use facial recognition technology to verify the identities of customers when they enter the bank and to detect and prevent fraud.
- *Payment*: Facial recognition technology is used in China for payment purposes. For example, customers can use their faces to pay for items at some stores or to access public transportation.
- *Education*: Some schools in China monitor students' attendance and behavior.
- *Transportation*: Facial recognition technology is also used in China for transportation purposes, such as to identify passengers boarding a train or to detect jaywalkers in busy intersections.

---

[3] For an outline, see Kostka, G., Steinacker, L., & Meckel, M. (2021). Between security and convenience: Facial recognition technology in the eyes of citizens in China, Germany, the United Kingdom, and the United States. *Public Understanding of Science, 30*(6), 671–690.

[4] For a review of non-government censorship, see Watters, P. A. (2020). Introduction: The Role of Censorship in Late Modern Societies. *Library Trends, 68*(4), 557–560.

[5] For a critical discussion, see Stark, R. (2021). China's use of artificial intelligence in their war against Xinjiang. *Tul. J. Int'l & Comp. L., 29*, 153

It's important to note that this is a topic of controversy, with concerns being raised about privacy violations and the potential for abuse by the government.[6]

China is not alone in this respect; surveillance has also increased and has been criticized in the United States, including:

1. *Police use*: Finding criminal suspects.
2. *Government surveillance*: For legitimate government surveillance, as well as the potential for the technology to be used for discriminatory purposes.
3. *Immigrant rights*: Facial recognition technology has been used at U.S. borders to identify and track individuals, raising concerns about the privacy and rights of immigrants and travelers.
4. *Civil rights*: There are concerns that facial recognition technology could be used for discriminatory purposes, such as profiling and tracking individuals based on race or ethnicity.

These concerns have led to calls for greater regulation by government agencies and greater transparency and accountability in the use of the technology. While some cities have banned these systems, they continue to be used by government agencies and private companies, with the debate over its use ongoing.

Audio

Audio surveillance refers to the act of monitoring and recording sounds and conversations through various means, including:

1. *Microphones*: Audio surveillance can be conducted using hidden or disguised microphones, which can be placed in a room or installed in electronic devices such as telephones or computers.
2. *Audio bugs*: Audio bugs are small, hidden devices that are designed especially for audio surveillance and can be concealed by an individual.
3. *Recording devices*: Audio surveillance can also be conducted using portable or fixed recording devices, such as dictaphones or digital voice recorders.
4. *Listening devices*: Some audio surveillance technologies, such as RF (radio frequency) bugs, are designed to be remotely monitored and allow the listener to hear audio in real-time.
5. *Software*: Audio surveillance can also be conducted using software, such as voice-over-IP (VoIP) monitoring tools, that allow for the recording and monitoring of audio conversations that take place over the internet.

The information gathered through audio surveillance may be used for criminal investigations, national security, and corporate espionage. The use of audio

---

[6] For a discussion, see Gurtov, M. (2021). US-China Relations and Human Rights: The Xinjiang Case. *Asian Perspective*, *45*(1), 83–90.

surveillance is often regulated by laws and guidelines but there is always a risk of misuse.[7]

In the cyber age, it is not necessary to physically plant a bug in a target premises – instead, it may be possible to remotely access a voice-activated virtual assistant. Amazon's Alexa is an example of such a virtual assistant that is integrated with many smart home devices. Alexa is designed to respond to voice commands and provide information and services; intelligence agencies and other bodies routinely engage in widespread surveillance of internet and telecommunications data and have the capability to access and monitor data collected by voice-activated virtual assistants like Alexa.

Like all internet-connected devices and services, Alexa may collect and store information about its users, including voice recordings and other data, which could potentially be accessed by the government through legal means, such as a court order or subpoena.

There have been instances where Amazon's Alexa voice data has been the subject of a search warrant or legal request, as part of criminal investigations or other legal proceedings.[8]

For example, in 2018, Amazon was compelled to turn over Alexa voice recordings as part of a murder investigation in Arkansas.[9] In another case, Amazon refused to comply with a search warrant for Alexa voice recordings in a murder case in Florida, citing concerns about user privacy.

There was a noteworthy European case study where Alexa data was misused, and it involves a case in Germany in 2019.[10]

In this case, a man named Daniel K. was charged with the murder of his girlfriend in their apartment. The police investigating the case obtained data from an Amazon Echo device that was in the apartment at the time of the murder. The device recorded sounds and conversations that took place in the apartment, including the moment of the murder.

The police obtained a warrant to access the data, which included recordings of the suspect arguing with his girlfriend and the sound of her screaming and being attacked. The Alexa device was activated by the sound of the attack and recorded the entire incident.

The case raised similar questions about the privacy implications of smart home devices and the potential misuse of the data they collect. The use of Alexa data in

---

[7] For a technical overview, see Liaquat, M. U., Munawar, H. S., Rahman, A., Qadir, Z., Kouzani, A. Z., & Mahmud, M. P. (2021). Localization of sound sources: A systematic review. *Energies*, *14*(13), 3910.

[8] For a review, see West, E. (2019). Amazon: Surveillance as a service. *Surveillance & Society*, *17*(1/2), 27–33.

[9] For details, see Merrill, M. (2019). An Uneasy Love Triangle Between Alexa, Your Personal Life, and Data Security: Exploring Privacy in the Digital New Age. *Mercer L. Rev.*, *71*, 637.

[10] For case details, see https://www.datenschutz-notizen.de/german-court-calls-alexa-to-the-stand-2028997/

this case was controversial, as it involved an invasion of the privacy of the victim, and there were concerns about the accuracy and reliability of the data.

However, in this case, the Alexa data played a critical role in securing a conviction, as the suspect's voice was captured on the recording, providing strong evidence of his involvement in the murder. The case highlighted the complex ethical and legal issues surrounding the use of data from smart home devices in criminal investigations and the need for clear guidelines and regulations to protect individuals' privacy rights.

These cases highlight the growing use of voice-activated virtual assistants like Alexa as sources of evidence in criminal investigations, and for intelligence purposes. Likewise, Voice over Internet Protocol (VoIP) traffic has also been subpoenaed in the United States as part of criminal investigations and legal proceedings. VoIP traffic, like other forms of digital communication, can be used as evidence in criminal cases and can be the subject of a subpoena or court order.

Web and Forum Surveillance

Surveillance on the World Wide Web can be undertaken in various ways, including:

- *Internet Service Provider (ISP) Monitoring*: Internet Service Providers can monitor their users' online activities through the data that passes through their servers.
- *Cookies*: Small pieces of data that can track browser behavior and gather information about their online activities.
- *Web Beacons*: Tiny code elements on websites that can be used to track user behavior.
- *Keyloggers*: Keyloggers are software programs that capture keystrokes, including passwords and other sensitive information.
- *Social Media Monitoring*: Social media platforms collect data on their users' activities, including the content they post, the pages they visit, and the people they interact with.
- *Government Surveillance*: Governments can use a variety of tools and techniques to monitor online activity, including wiretapping, hacking, and data collection programs.
- *Online Advertising*: Online advertising companies can collect information about users' online activities through tracking pixels and other tracking technologies.[11]

A common example of government surveillance of criminals might involve monitoring chat rooms (or forums). A chat forum, also known as an online discussion forum, is a platform that enables users to engage in online conversations with one

---

[11] For a case study, see Watters, P. A., Watters, M. F., & Ziegler, J. (2015, January). Maximising eyeballs but facilitating cybercrime? ethical challenges for online advertising in new zealand. In *2015 48th Hawaii International Conference on System Sciences* (pp. 1742–1749). IEEE.

another. These forums are typically organized around specific topics or interests, and users can post messages, ask questions, and respond to others.

Chat forums are usually organized into threads, with each thread focusing on a specific topic. Users can start new threads or contribute to existing ones, and the conversations can continue over a period, often resulting in a rich and diverse exchange of ideas and opinions.

Chat forums can be moderated, meaning that a moderator or a team of moderators can review and approve posts before they are published, or unmoderated, meaning that posts are published immediately without any review.

Chat forums can be found on various websites, including news websites, social media platforms, and specialized forums dedicated to specific interests or industries. They can be a valuable resource for people looking to connect with others who share their interests, seek advice, or simply engage in lively discussions.

Chat forums can be used by criminals as well as non-criminals. Like any other online platform, chat forums can be used for exploitation by those with malicious intent, including cybercriminals, scammers, hackers, and so on.

Criminals can use chat forums to communicate with one another, share information and resources, and plan illegal activities. For example, they may use chat forums to exchange stolen credit card information, plan cyber-attacks, or discuss illegal drug trafficking.

One noteworthy case study where chat forums have been monitored leading to prosecution is the Silk Road where an "Aladdin's cave" of illicit drugs were bought and sold using Bitcoin.[12]

In this case, the investigation into the Silk Road involved monitoring online chat forums and other forms of online communication. The investigation was led by the FBI, which used a range of techniques to track down Ulbricht and other members of the Silk Road.

One of the key pieces of evidence in the case was a collection of online chat logs that were obtained by the FBI. These logs contained conversations between Ulbricht and other members of the Silk Road, which were used to build a case against him.

The chat logs included discussions of illegal activities, including drug trafficking and money laundering, as well as conversations about the administration of the Silk Road website. The FBI also used other forms of surveillance, such as monitoring Bitcoin transactions, to track down the individuals involved in the operation.[13]

Ulbricht was eventually arrested and charged with a range of offenses, including drug trafficking, money laundering, and computer hacking, and was later jailed.

---

[12] For a review, see Frank, R., & Mikhaylov, A. (2020). Beyond the 'Silk Road': Assessing illicit drug marketplaces on the public web. *Open Source Intelligence and Cyber Crime: Social Media Analytics*, 89–111.

[13] Not all drug trafficking occurs on the dark web, for examples, see Watters, P. A., & Phair, N. (2012). Detecting illicit drugs on social media using automated social media intelligence analysis (ASMIA). In *Cyberspace Safety and Security: 4th International Symposium, CSS 2012, Melbourne, Australia, December 12–13, 2012. Proceedings 4* (pp. 66–76). Springer Berlin Heidelberg.

The case of Ross Ulbricht and the Silk Road highlights the importance of monitoring online communication in the investigation of online criminal activity.

There are various techniques that can be used to monitor chat forums for criminal activity. Some of the common techniques are:

- *Keyword Monitoring*: Law enforcement agencies may use keyword monitoring tools to scan chat forums for specific words or phrases that are associated with criminal activity. These tools can help identify potentially suspicious conversations and alert law enforcement to investigate further.
- *Data Mining*: Data mining involves using software to assess vasy quantities of data to find patterns of interest. Law enforcement agencies typically use data mining tools to analyze chat forum data and identify potential criminal activity.[14]
- *User Profiling*: User profiling involves creating profiles of chat forum users based on their behavior, interests, and other characteristics. Law enforcement agencies may use user profiling to identify individuals who are likely to be involved in criminal activity and to target their investigations accordingly.
- *Network Analysis*: Network analysis involves mapping out the relationships between chat forum users to identify potential criminal networks. Law enforcement agencies may use network analysis tools to identify individuals who are connected to known criminal organizations or who are involved in illegal activities.
- *Human Intelligence*: Human intelligence involves using trained personnel to monitor chat forums and identify potential criminal activity. Law enforcement agencies may use human intelligence to supplement automated monitoring tools and gather additional information about potential criminal activity.

In summary, the goal of monitoring chat forums for criminal activity is to identify potential threats and take appropriate action to prevent or investigate criminal activity. It is important for these monitoring techniques to be used ethically and with proper oversight to protect the privacy and civil liberties of chat forum users.

Here is an example of how keyword monitoring can be used to identify potential criminal activity on a chat forum:

Let's say that law enforcement is monitoring a chat forum where discussions related to illegal drug trafficking have been reported. To identify potential criminal activity, law enforcement may use keyword monitoring tools to scan the forum for specific words or phrases that are associated with drug trafficking, such as "cocaine," "marijuana," "heroin," "drug deal," "drug smuggling," and so on.

When the keyword monitoring tool detects these keywords or phrases, it can flag the messages for further investigation by law enforcement. For example, if a user posts a message that contains the phrase "I just got a shipment of cocaine," the keyword monitoring tool will flag this message as potentially suspicious.

---

[14] For an analysis of requirements for large-scale monitoring, see Camp, L. J., Grobler, M., Jang-Jaccard, J., Probst, C., Renaud, K., & Watters, P. (2019). Measuring human resilience in the face of the global epidemiology of cyber attacks.

Law enforcement can then review the flagged messages and determine if further investigation is warranted. If the message appears to be indicative of criminal activity, law enforcement may take action to investigate the user and any potential criminal networks they may be involved in.[15]

Keyword monitoring can be an effective way to identify potential criminal activity on chat forums. However, it is important for law enforcement to use these tools ethically and with proper oversight to ensure that the privacy and civil liberties of chat forum users are protected.[16]

Data mining can be used to improve the accuracy and performance of keyword monitoring by identifying patterns and trends in chat forum data that may not be immediately apparent through manual keyword monitoring.

One way that data mining can be used is by analyzing the frequency and co-occurrence of certain keywords and phrases within chat forum conversations. This analysis can help identify common themes and topics that are associated with criminal activity. For example, data mining may reveal that certain drug-related keywords tend to co-occur with specific geographic locations, indicating potential hotspots for drug trafficking.

Let's say that law enforcement is monitoring a chat forum that is known to be used by drug traffickers. They have identified several drug-related keywords, including "cocaine," "heroin," "marijuana," and "drug deal," that they are monitoring for. However, they want to use data mining to find patterns and trends in the chat forum data which may be difficult to find through manual keyword monitoring.

Through data mining, law enforcement can analyze the frequency and co-occurrence of these keywords and phrases within chat forum conversations. For example, they may find that the keyword "cocaine" tends to co-occur with the keywords "Miami," "Colombia," and "shipment." This could indicate that there is a high frequency of cocaine trafficking originating from Miami and/or Colombia, and that there may be a specific shipment being discussed in the chat forum.

Alternatively, law enforcement may find that the keyword "heroin" tends to co-occur with the keywords "Chicago," "distributor," and "price." This could indicate that there is a specific heroin distributor operating in Chicago and that chat forum users are discussing the price of heroin sold by this distributor.

Network analysis could potentially be used to complement the frequency and co-occurrence analysis of certain keywords and phrases within chat forum conversations by identifying the relationships between users and the structure of the chat forum.

---

[15] For an ethical overview, see Watters, P., Scolyer-Gray, P., Kayes, A. S. M., & Chowdhury, M. J. M. (2019). This would work perfectly if it weren't for all the humans: Two factor authentication in late modern societies. *First Monday*.

[16] Plus, keyword monitoring can be unreliable, for details, see Ho, W. H., & Watters, P. A. (2004, October). Statistical and structural approaches to filtering internet pornography. In *2004 IEEE International Conference on Systems, Man and Cybernetics (IEEE Cat. No. 04CH37583)* (Vol. 5, pp. 4792–4798). IEEE.

For example, network analysis can be used to identify which users are most active in drug-related discussions and who they are communicating with. It can also reveal which users are central to the network, meaning that they have connections to many other users in the network, and which users are on the periphery, meaning that they have few connections.

By combining network analysis with keyword analysis, law enforcement can identify not only the most active drug-related discussions but also the most influential users and groups within the chat forum. They can then focus their efforts on these users and groups to gather further evidence and disrupt drug trafficking activities.

Social Network Aanalysis (SNA) is one specific method for studying social structures using network and graph theories.[17]

One way to apply SNA in the context of chat forums is to analyze the patterns of interactions between users. This can involve constructing a network graph that represents the relationships between users based on their interactions. In such a network, each user is represented by a node, and each interaction between users is represented by an edge.

Using this network graph, we can calculate various network metrics that can provide insight into the communication patterns within the forum. For example, we can calculate degree centrality and related measures to identify users who are likely to be influential within the network and may alter the flow of data and discussions within the forum.

We can also calculate other metrics to identify intermediaries who may play a crucial role in facilitating communication between different groups of users.

Other metrics that can be calculated include eigenvector centrality and the clustering coefficient. By using SNA to analyze chat forums, we can gain a deeper understanding of the communication patterns and social structures within the forum, which can be useful for identifying influential users, and understanding the flow of information.

Another way that data mining can be used is by identifying unusual activity or behavior patterns within chat forum conversations. For example, data mining may reveal that a specific user tends to use a high number of drug-related keywords, indicating potential involvement in drug trafficking. This user can then be flagged for further investigation.

Data mining can also be used to identify changes in language and communication patterns over time. For example, data mining may reveal that a new slang term is being used in chat forum conversations to refer to a specific drug, indicating a shift in the drug trafficking landscape.

However, there are some fundamental limitations to the use of large graphs,[18] data mining and social network analysis, including:

---

[17] For an outline, see Van der Hulst, R. C. (2009). Introduction to Social Network Analysis (SNA) as an investigative tool. *Trends in Organized Crime, 12*, 101–121.

[18] For an outline of the theoretical background, see Dekker, A., Pérez-Rosés, H., Pineda-Villavicencio, G., & Watters, P. (2012). The maximum degree & diameter-bounded subgraph and

- *Scalability*: Network size and cost are strongly linked. This makes it difficult to analyze very large social networks with many connections.
- *Sampling bias*: For large social networks, it may be difficult to obtain a representative sample of the entire network. This can lead to sampling bias and inaccurate results.
- *Sparsity*: Many social networks have a sparse structure, where the majority of nodes have only a few connections. This can make it difficult to identify important nodes and communities within the network.
- *Complexity*: Large social networks can exhibit complex patterns of connections, including clustering, assortativity, and hierarchical structure. These patterns can be difficult to detect and interpret using traditional network analysis methods.
- *Dynamic nature*: Social networks are dynamic, meaning that they evolve and change over time. This can make it difficult to analyze the network at a single point in time and requires the use of dynamic network analysis methods.

SNA is also related to the concept of "six degrees of separation" in that both are concerned with the connections and relationships between individuals in a network, with no more than six intermediaries, meaning that everyone is linked to everyone else through a small number of connections.[19] This idea gained widespread attention after it was popularized by a play and later a movie of the same name.

Social network analysis provides a framework for studying these connections and relationships in more detail. SNA examines the structure of social networks and identifies patterns of connections, such as clusters of densely interconnected individuals or important nodes that act as bridges between different parts of the network.

By analyzing the structure of social networks, SNA can provide insights into how information, influence, and other resources flow through the network. This can help explain why some individuals are more influential or connected than others and can inform strategies for targeting key individuals or groups in the network.

Overall, both six degrees of separation and SNA are concerned with understanding the complex web of relationships that connect people and shape social interactions.

Summary

By using data mining to supplement keyword monitoring, law enforcement can improve the accuracy and performance of their monitoring efforts and identify potential criminal activity more effectively. The use of Data Mining and Artificial Intelligence and associated techniques, and the methodological considerations therein, are covered in Chap. 8.

---

its applications. *Journal of Mathematical Modelling and Algorithms*, *11*, 249–268.

[19] For a critique, read Kleinfeld, J. (2002). Could it be a big world after all? The six degrees of separation myth. *Society, April*, *12*, 5–2.

Chapter 8
Data Analysis

Data analysis is important in counterintelligence because it allows intelligence agencies to collect information about threats or vulnerabilities, and make sensible and valid characterizations or predictions.

Counterintelligence involves detecting and neutralizing threats posed by foreign intelligence services, terrorist organizations, or other hostile entities. These threats may come in various forms, such as espionage, cyber-attacks, or sabotage. To effectively counter these threats, intelligence agencies need to find data from a wide variety of sources, including signals intelligence, human intelligence, and open-source intelligence.

Data analysis is important in this context for several reasons:

- *Identifying patterns and anomalies*: By analyzing datasets, intelligence agencies can find markers of suspicious activity or behavior. For example, they may detect a sudden increase in cyber-attacks from a particular country, or a pattern of suspicious financial transactions that may be linked to terrorist financing.
- *Predictive analysis*: Data analysis can help intelligence agencies to predict future threats or attacks by identifying trends and patterns that may indicate future behavior. For example, they may detect an increase in chatter or communication among terrorist groups that suggests an imminent attack.[1]
- *Identifying vulnerabilities*: Data analysis can also help intelligence agencies to identify vulnerabilities in their own operations or systems that may be exploited by hostile entities. By analyzing data on past attacks or espionage attempts, they can identify common tactics and weaknesses that may be targeted in the future.

---

[1]For a technical architecture, see Azab, A., Maruatona, O., & Watters, P. (2019). AVOCAD: Adaptive terrorist comms surveillance and interception using machine learning. In *2019 18th IEEE International Conference On Trust, Security And Privacy In Computing And Communications*, pp. 85–94. IEEE.

P. A. Watters, *Counterintelligence in a Cyber World*,
https://doi.org/10.1007/978-3-031-35287-4_8

In this chapter, these three elements will be further expanded with a view to understanding how novel technologies such as AI and ML can be developed and applied to solve classic counterintelligence problems.

Pattern Recognition and Anomaly Detection

Pattern recognition is the process of identifying and classifying patterns or structures in data. It involves the use of mathematical algorithms and statistical methods to analyze and detect changes or characteristics not immediately apparent to even a trained eye.

An important upfront distinction is made between supervised and unsupervised learning for pattern recognition. Supervised learning uses known cases or labels. This means that the model is trained with input variables (also called features) as well as the correct output variables (or labels). The relationship between input and output is "learned", allowing new predictions to be made. Examples of supervised algorithms include classification, regression, and time series analysis.[2]

In contrast, unsupervised learning only uses unlabeled data. This requires only includes input variables (features) and does not include output variables (labels). The model uses this unlabeled data to find new insights within the data and can then group similar data points together or identify anomalies that may be present. Typical algorithms in this category include cluster analysis, anomaly detection, and dimensionality reduction.[3]

Below is an example of how dimensionality reduction can be used in the context of security data:

Suppose we have a large dataset containing various security events (such as malware detection,[4] network intrusions, or logins) for a particular system. Each event is represented by many features, such as the user or device involved, the IP addresses and ports used, and various other metadata.

If we wanted to perform analysis on this dataset, we would need to deal with the high dimensionality of the data, which could make it difficult to visualize or analyze effectively. We can utilize dimensionality reduction to reduce feature and matrix sizes by mapping into a smaller space. Orthogonally, the easiest way to do this is via Factor Analysis (FA), or Principal Component Analysis (PCA). The resulting

---

[2] For a malware case study, see Alazab, M., Venkatraman, S., Watters, P. A., & Alazab, M. (2011). Zero-day Malware Detection based on Supervised Learning Algorithms of API call Signatures. *AusDM, 11*, 171–182.

[3] For a pertinent example, see Layton, R., Watters, P., & Dazeley, R. (2013). Automated unsupervised authorship analysis using evidence accumulation clustering. *Natural Language Engineering, 19*(1), 95–120.

[4] For some technical background, see Zhu, J., Jang-Jaccard, J., & Watters, P. A. (2020). Multi-loss Siamese neural network with batch normalization layer for malware detection. *IEEE Access, 8*, 171542–171550.

orthogonal feature sets are quite easy to interpret, assuming that a large enough proportion of the variance can be captured.

To illustrate this, let's assume we have a dataset with 100 features and 1000 security events. We can use PCA to extract, say, 10 orthogonal components. This would allow us to represent each event with only 10 features, while still capturing a significant amount of the variance in the original data.

Once we have reduced the dimensionality of the data, we can then perform various types of analysis or visualization to gain insights into the security events. For example, we could cluster the events based on their reduced feature representations to identify patterns or anomalies in the data. We could also perform classification or prediction tasks using the reduced features as inputs.[5]

Pattern recognition is a key component of many fields, including computer science. It is utilized to analyze, find and classify a wide range of data, including images, speech, and text.

In pattern recognition, data is typically represented as feature sets or attributes that describe pattern characteristics. These can be drawn out using various methods, like image processing techniques or natural language processing algorithms.

Once the features have been extracted, a pattern recognition system is used to classify the data into different categories. This classification is based on the relationships between the features and the patterns they represent. A range of algorithms have been developed by computer scientists to support pattern recognition, some of which are biologically inspired.

Pattern recognition has many applications, including image and speech recognition, handwriting recognition, fraud detection, and medical diagnosis. In each of these applications, pattern recognition algorithms are used to identify and classify patterns or structures.

Pattern recognition can be a useful tool in counterintelligence for identifying patterns and anomalies that may indicate suspicious activity or behavior. By analyzing significant data volumes, intelligence agencies can identify patterns that may be associated with espionage, terrorism, or other threats.

Described below are some examples of how pattern recognition can be used in counterintelligence:

- *Network analysis*: Intelligence agencies can use pattern recognition to analyze communication networks between individuals and organizations to identify suspicious patterns of communication. For example, they may detect an unusual increase in the frequency or volume of communications between certain individuals, or a sudden shift in the type of communication used (such as a shift from phone calls to encrypted messaging).
- *Financial analysis*: Pattern recognition can assess financial transactions to find links and trends. For example, intelligence agencies may detect patterns of suspi-

---

[5] For a theoretical analysis, see Kelarev, A. V., Yearwood, J. L., & Watters, P. A. (2011, April). Optimization of classifiers for data mining based on combinatorial semigroups. In *Semigroup Forum* (Vol. 82, pp. 242–251). Springer-Verlag.

cious transactions involving certain individuals or organizations, or patterns of transactions that deviate significantly from normal patterns of financial behavior.

- *Cybersecurity*: Pattern recognition can be used to detect patterns of suspicious activity in computer networks that may indicate cyber-attacks or other threats. For example, intelligence agencies may detect patterns of traffic that are associated with malware or hacking attempts, or patterns of activity that suggest an attempt to hack a host.

One of the main threats in cybersecurity is using malware to steal information. To detect malware, intelligence agencies can use pattern recognition algorithms to find patterns of behavior linked to malware.

For example, intelligence agencies may use software to find behavioral activity associated with different types of malware. They can easily distinguish between malware and non-malicious characteristics, and can also learn to get better at their job.

Once the algorithm has been trained, real-time data can be used for detecting patterns that are associated with malware. For example, the algorithm may detect patterns of traffic that are associated with the download and installation of malware, or patterns of traffic that suggest that a system has been compromised.

By using pattern recognition to detect malware, intelligence agencies can stay ahead of emerging threats and take proactive steps to mitigate them. They can also use the patterns identified by the algorithm to develop new cybersecurity measures that are more effective at detecting and preventing malware attacks.

Three commonly used algorithms for pattern recognition and malware detection:

- *Support Vector Machines (SVMs)*: SVMs can be used for regression analysis and related purposes by identifying a decision boundary which is defined to separate different classes of data. SVMs have been shown to be effective for malware detection, particularly when used in combination with other techniques such as feature selection and ensemble methods.
- *Random Forests*: Random Forests implement classification combining a range of decision tree outputs to make a final prediction. Random Forests are particularly effective for dealing with noisy or incomplete data and have been shown to be effective for malware detection.
- *Deep Learning*: Deep Learning algorithms work by creating multiple layers of interconnected nodes that can learn to recognize complex patterns in data. Deep Learning has shown promising results in malware detection, particularly when used in combination with other techniques such as dynamic analysis and behavior-based detection. Deep learning also requires significant volumes of data and computational resources, that make it challenging for implementation in some applications.

In summary, the choice of algorithm for pattern recognition and malware detection will depend on factors such as the complexity of the data, the specific application, and the resources available for analysis. It is often necessary to use a combination of different algorithms and techniques to achieve the best results.

Supervised learning has been used in various ways to analyze malware. One common application is to use supervised learning algorithms to build malware detection systems.

In this approach, a dataset of known malware samples is used to train a supervised learning algorithm, such as a decision tree, random forest, or neural network, to recognize patterns or features in the malware code that distinguish it from benign software. The algorithm can then be used to scan new software for these patterns and identify whether it is likely to be malware.

Another way that supervised learning has been used to analyze malware is in malware classification.[6] In this approach, a dataset of malware samples is labeled with information about its behavior, such as whether it is a Trojan, virus, or worm. This labeled dataset is then used to train software to identify new malware samples using observations of their behavior.

Finally, supervised learning has also been used to characterize malware for zero-days. In this approach, a supervised learning algorithm is trained on a dataset of known malware behaviors, and then used to monitor software in real-time for any suspicious behavior that matches the known malware behaviors.

Overall, the use of supervised learning in malware analysis has helped improve the accuracy and efficiency of malware detection and classification and has enabled faster and more effective response to malware threats.

Regarding the use of clustering and malware,[7] analyzing the number of natural groupings (clusters) of malware that have been found by research depends on a variety of factors, such as the methods and criteria used for clustering, the size and diversity of the dataset being analyzed, and the goals and objectives of the research.

There have been many research studies that have used clustering techniques to group malware samples into clusters based on various characteristics, such as code similarity, behavior patterns, or temporal relationships.[8] These studies have identified anywhere from a few dozen to tens of thousands of clusters of malware, depending on the scope and scale of the analysis.

It's important to note that clustering malware samples into groups can be a challenging task,[9] as malware authors often use various obfuscation techniques to make

---

[6] For an example, see Black, P., Sohail, A., Gondal, I., Kamruzzaman, J., Vamplew, P., & Watters, P. (2020). API based discrimination of ransomware and benign cryptographic programs. In *Neural Information Processing: 27th International Conference, ICONIP 2020, Bangkok, Thailand, November 23–27, 2020, Proceedings, Part II 27* (pp. 177–188). Springer International Publishing.

[7] For an empirical study, see Mosharrat, N., Sarker, I. H., Anwar, M. M., Islam, M. N., Watters, P., & Hammoudeh, M. (2022). Automatic Malware Categorization Based on K-Means Clustering Technique. In *Proceedings of the International Conference on Big Data, IoT, and Machine Learning: BIM 2021* (pp. 653–664). Springer Singapore.

[8] For an in-depth analysis, see Kelarev, A. V., Yearwood, J. L., Watters, P. A., Wu, X., Ma, L., Abawajy, J. H., & Pan, L. (2011). A Groebner-Shirshov algorithm for applications in internet security. *Southeast Asian Bulletin of Mathematics*, *36*(1), 87–100.

[9] For an explanation, see Edem, E. I., Benzaïd, C., Al-Nemrat, A., & Watters, P. (2014). Analysis of malware behaviour: Using data mining clustering techniques to support forensics investigation. In *2014 Fifth Cybercrime and Trustworthy Computing Conference* (pp. 54–63). IEEE.

their code and behavior patterns difficult to detect and analyze. Additionally, different malware families can share similar code or behavior patterns, making it challenging to distinguish between them. As such, the results of clustering analyses should be interpreted with caution and may vary depending on the specific clustering method and dataset being used.

What actually is clustering? Cluster analysis uses features to group together cases which share some kind of similarity. It partitions a set of data points into a smaller number of groups (clusters) based on their similarities.[10]

There are several different methods of cluster analysis, but they all involve calculating likeness between cases and grouping them accordingly, typically using a distance metric. Once the distance matrix is calculated, the clustering algorithm starts grouping the objects into clusters, using a hierarchical or non-hierarchical approach.

Hierarchical clustering algorithms build a pyramid, starting from the individual data points then grouping them together into larger and larger clusters. This process can be visualized using a dendrogram, which shows the hierarchy of clusters.

Non-hierarchical clustering algorithms, also known as partitional clustering algorithms, do not create a hierarchy of clusters. Instead, they directly partition the data into a pre-specified number of clusters, which is the case for k-means, probably the most commonly used clustering algorithm of all time. Cluster analysis is a useful technique for exploring and summarizing large datasets, identifying meaningful patterns, and reducing the dimensionality of data.

An important qualification is anomalies in the interpretation of this kind of result. Anomalies can play an important role in data analysis for counterintelligence, as they may indicate potential threats or risks that require further investigation. An anomaly is any deviation from the expected behavior or pattern in a dataset, which may be caused by a variety of factors such as errors, fraud, or malicious activity.[11]

In the context of counterintelligence, anomalies may indicate a variety of potential threats or risks, such as:

- *Cyber-attacks*: Anomalies in network traffic or log files may indicate that a system has been compromised or is under attack by hackers.
- *Insider threats*: Anomalies in employee behavior, such as accessing sensitive data outside of normal working hours, may indicate that an employee is engaged in espionage or sabotage.
- *Terrorism*: Anomalies in travel patterns or financial transactions may indicate that an individual or group is planning a terrorist attack.
- *Espionage*: Anomalies in communication patterns or data access may indicate that a foreign intelligence agency is attempting to steal sensitive information.

---

[10] For a computational example, see Watters, P. A. (2002). Discriminating English word senses using cluster analysis. *Journal of Quantitative Linguistics*, 9(1), 77–86.

[11] For an example, see Lee, S. J., & Watters, P. A. (2017, July). Cyber budget optimization through security event clustering. In *2017 IEEE 7th Annual International Conference on CYBER Technology in Automation, Control, and Intelligent Systems (CYBER)* (pp. 1026–1031). IEEE.

By using data analysis techniques to detect anomalies in large volumes of data, counterintelligence agencies can gain early warning of potential threats and take action to prevent them. Techniques such as anomaly detection algorithms, clustering, and network analysis can learn from historical data and predict future anomalies.

A related concept is false positives. Anomalies and false positives are related in that both refer to unexpected results that may be generated by data analysis techniques.

An anomaly is any deviation from the expected behavior or pattern in a dataset, which may be caused by errors, fraud, or malicious activity.[12] Anomalies are often detected using statistical techniques that identify patterns and outliers in data.

A false positive, on the other hand, is a result that is generated by a data analysis technique but is not actually true. For example, a machine learning algorithm may generate a false positive when it predicts that a benign event is actually malicious.

In the context of data analysis for counterintelligence, false positives can be a significant problem, as they can lead to unnecessary investigations or actions, wasting valuable resources and potentially damaging the reputation of innocent individuals. For example, a false positive in a network intrusion detection system may trigger an alarm and lead to an investigation, even though no actual intrusion has occurred.

Anomalies can sometimes be mistaken for false positives, particularly if the anomaly detection technique is not well-tuned or if the data is noisy. However, anomalies can also be genuine indicators of potential threats or risks, and as such, it is important to carefully evaluate each anomaly to determine whether it represents a true positive or a false positive.

False positives in the context of counterintelligence can have serious consequences if they lead to incorrect or unjustified actions, particularly if these actions result in harm to innocent individuals or damage to national security.

For example, a false positive in a terrorist threat detection system could result in an innocent individual being detained or subjected to additional security checks, leading to a violation of their civil liberties, and potentially damaging the reputation of law enforcement or intelligence agencies. In extreme cases, false positives may also divert attention and resources away from genuine threats, leaving the country vulnerable to attack.

It is therefore essential for counterintelligence agencies to carefully evaluate the reliability and accuracy of their data analysis techniques, and to minimize the risk of false positives by using robust validation and testing procedures, as well as human intelligence and judgement to verify results before taking any action.

---

[12] For a review, see Maruatona, O., Vamplew, P., Dazeley, R., & Watters, P. A. (2017). Evaluating accuracy in prudence analysis for cyber security. In *Neural Information Processing: 24th International Conference, ICONIP 2017, Guangzhou, China, November 14–18, 2017, Proceedings, Part V 24* (pp. 407–417). Springer International Publishing.

A relevant example is that of Xi Xiaoxing[13] who had espionage charges against him dropped. The real-world consequences of false positives for the individuals concerned are severe: loss of income/job, loss of status/reputation, and being branded a spy.

On the flip side is the case of FBI agent Robert Hanssen, found to be a Russian spy. Despite being investigated multiple times by the FBI's security division, Hanssen was able to avoid detection and continue his espionage activities for years.[14]

One reason for this failure was that Hanssen did not exhibit many of the typical "anomalies" that might indicate someone is engaging in espionage, such as financial problems, substance abuse, or erratic behavior. Instead, he was seen as a model employee and family man, which may have led investigators to overlook warning signs.

Another example is the case of NSA contractor Edward Snowden, who leaked classified information about the US government's surveillance activities. Despite working in a highly secure environment with strict access controls and monitoring, Snowden was able to bypass these safeguards and access sensitive information without raising suspicion.

Again, Snowden did not exhibit many of the typical anomalies that might indicate someone is engaging in espionage, and his actions were not detected by standard monitoring systems. Instead, he exploited vulnerabilities in the system and used his technical skills and knowledge of the system to evade detection.

These cases highlight the limitations of relying solely on anomaly detection in counterintelligence efforts.[15] While anomaly detection can be a useful tool, it is not foolproof, and sophisticated adversaries may be able to evade detection by avoiding typical warning signs or exploiting vulnerabilities in the system.

Predictive Analysis

Predictive analysis is simply tries to make accurate predictions about future events. Historical data is utilized to train an algorithm, which is then used to make predictions about future events. The model is typically trained using a subset of the data, and its accuracy is evaluated using a different subset of the data.

Predictive analysis is used across a lot of domains, including cybersecurity, among others. For example, predictive analysis can be used to forecast future sales

---

[13] For a description of the case, see https://www.newyorker.com/news/news-desk/the-spy-who-was-innocent

[14] For a review, see Blackman, A., & Shannon, E. (2008). *The spy next door: The extraordinary secret life of Robert Philip Hanssen, the most damaging FBI agent in US history*. Hachette UK.

[15] For a mathematical analysis, see Pasquinelli, M. (2015). Anomaly detection: The mathematization of the abnormal in the metadata society. *Panel presentation at Transmediale Festival, Berlin, Germany*.

trends, identify customers who are at risk of leaving, predict disease outbreaks, or detect anomalies in network traffic.

In summary, predictive analysis is a powerful tool for extracting insights and making choices using those insights. It has many practical applications across a wide range of domains and is likely to become increasingly important as data continues to play an increasingly central role in business and society.

Predictive analytics can be used for counterintelligence to identify potential threats and risks, and to anticipate and prevent future attacks. Described below are some ways that predictive analytics can be applied in the context of counterintelligence:

- *Threat detection*: Predictive analytics works from multiple sources, such as social media, communication networks, and public records, using clustering and classification to detect trends. Thus, counterintelligence agencies can gain early warning of potential attacks and take action to prevent them.
- *Risk assessment*: Predictive analytics can be used to assess the risk of different individuals or groups, based on factors such as their past behavior, affiliations, and travel history. By combining insights from multiple sources, counterintelligence agencies can identify high-risk individuals and groups and take steps to mitigate the threat they pose.
- *Insider threat detection*: Predictive analytics can be used to detect potential offenders that may be planning to commit sabotage or related activities. By examining employee email and network activity, counterintelligence agencies can identify patterns of behavior that may indicate a potential insider threat.
- *Cybersecurity*: Predictive analytics may find signatures of potential cyber-attacks, by assessing network traffic, log files, and other data. By using advanced software to analyze data in real-time, counterintelligence agencies can detect and respond to cyber-attacks quickly before they can cause significant damage.

Below is an example of how predictive analytics could be used for risk assessment in the context of counterintelligence: Let's say a counterintelligence agency wants to assess the risk posed by a particular individual who has recently come to their attention. They have access to a variety of data sources, including social media profiles, financial records, and travel history.

1. *Data collection*: The first step is to gather data and ensure that it is clean and complete. For example, the agency may collect data on the individual's social media activity, financial transactions, and travel history.
2. *Feature selection and engineering*: Identify the most relevant data features, and engineer new features that may be useful for predicting risk. For example, the agency may extract features such as the individual's social media activity (number of posts, likes, and comments), financial transactions (amount, frequency, and destination), and travel history (destination, duration, and frequency).
3. *Model selection and training*: Once the features have been selected and engineered, the agency can train a model to estimate the individual's risk level. The agency may choose from a wide range of models as dictated by the specific

algorithmic and data requirements. After subset is used for training, agencies can then use techniques such as cross-validation to ensure that it is accurate and reliable.

4. *Evaluation and optimization*: After the model has been trained, the agency evaluates its performance on a different subset of the data, using a range of metrics. If the model's performance is not satisfactory, the agency can refine the feature selection and engineering, try different machine learning algorithms, or collect additional data to improve the model's accuracy.

Once the model has been trained and evaluated, the agency can use it to predict the risk level of new individuals based on their social media activity, financial transactions, and travel history. For example, if the model predicts a high-risk level for an individual, the agency may choose to conduct further investigations, such as monitoring their communications or conducting interviews with associates.

One example of using predictive analytics for risk assessment in the context of counterintelligence is the Insider Threat Program (ITP) implemented by the US government. The ITP is designed to identify individuals within government agencies who may pose a threat to national security by leaking sensitive information or engaging in espionage.

The ITP uses a range of data sources, including financial records, employee performance evaluations, and social media, looking for behaviors which might suggest a heightened risk of insider threat. Predictive analytics is used to analyze this data and identify individuals who may be at risk of becoming an insider threat.

For example, if an employee with access to classified information suddenly exhibits a pattern of financial difficulties or has a sudden increase in online activity related to foreign countries, the ITP may flag this behavior as a potential risk for insider threat. Similarly, if an employee exhibits a pattern of security violations or unexplained absences, the ITP may investigate further to determine if there is a risk of insider threat.

The ITP has been credited with helping to prevent several high-profile cases of insider threat, including the case of Chelsea Manning, and the case of Harold Martin, a former National Security Agency contractor who was found to have stolen classified information.[16]

Predicting cyber-attacks can be a challenging task because of a range of factors. However, there are several techniques that can be used to detect and predict potential attacks:

- *Machine Learning*: These algorithms are trained on historical data to indicate risk. This can be achieved using techniques such as anomaly detection, as described above.

---

[16]For a review, see Christensen, C. (2014). A decade of WikiLeaks: So what?. *International Journal of Media & Cultural Politics*, *10*(3), 273–284.

- *Threat Intelligence*: This involves collecting and analyzing data on known threats and attackers. This data can be used to predict potential attacks based on similarities to previous attacks.
- *Behavioral Analysis*: Behavioral analysis involves monitoring system and user behavior to identify unusual activity that may indicate an attack. This can be done using techniques such as user behavior analytics and network traffic analysis.
- *Vulnerability Scanning*: Vulnerability scanning involves identifying vulnerabilities in systems and applications that can be exploited by attackers. By proactively identifying and patching vulnerabilities, potential attacks can be prevented.
- *Human Expertise*: Cybersecurity experts can use their knowledge and experience to identify potential attack vectors and develop strategies to mitigate them. This may involve monitoring industry-specific trends and threat actors, as well as staying up to date with the latest security technologies.

Identifying Vulnerabilities

There are many operations or systems that can be exploited by hostile entities that can be revealed through data analysis. One noteworthy case of system exploitation that was revealed through data analysis is the 2013 Target data breach. In this attack, hackers gained access to Target's payment system, gaining access to personal data of many Americans.

Through data analysis, it was revealed that the attackers were able to hack into the Target point-of-sale (POS) systems. Specifically, they were able to install malware on the POS systems that allowed them to intercept and steal payment card information as it was being processed.[17]

This attack demonstrates the importance of data analysis in detecting and preventing cyber-attacks. By analyzing the payment card data that was stolen, investigators were able to identify patterns that indicated a potential breach. For example, they noticed that the stolen card data was being sold on underground marketplaces, suggesting that the attackers were motivated by financial gain.

Through further analysis, investigators were able to identify the specific malware used in the attack and trace it back to a malicious emails targeting a Target contractor, facilitating access ultimately to Target's network.

Described below are some further examples:

- *Insider Threats*: Hostile entities can exploit vulnerabilities in the system by recruiting insiders to steal sensitive data or perform other malicious activities. Data analysis may reveal behaviors indicative of the presence of an insider threat,

---

[17] For a review, see Cheng, L., Liu, F., & Yao, D. (2017). Enterprise data breach: causes, challenges, prevention, and future directions. *Wiley Interdisciplinary Reviews: Data Mining and Knowledge Discovery*, 7(5), e1211.

such as sudden changes in the amount or type of data being accessed by an employee.

- *Cybersecurity Vulnerabilities*: Hostile entities can exploit vulnerabilities in the system by targeting weaknesses in cybersecurity protocols. Data analysis can help to identify patterns of attacks and the types of vulnerabilities that are being exploited, which can inform the development of more effective cybersecurity measures.
- *Supply Chain Vulnerabilities*: Hostile entities can exploit vulnerabilities in the supply chain by targeting third-party vendors or suppliers that have access to sensitive data or systems. Data analysis can help to identify potential vulnerabilities in the supply chain and inform decisions about which vendors or suppliers to use.
- *Communication Channels*: Hostile entities can exploit vulnerabilities in communication channels to intercept or manipulate sensitive information. Data analysis of communication patterns may be indicative of the presence of a compromise, such as unusual traffic or patterns of communication.

In summary, data analysis can be a valuable tool in identifying vulnerabilities that can be exploited by hostile entities.

One example of how vulnerabilities have been exploited in counterintelligence is Edward Snowden's case from 2013 involving the NSA. Snowden's actions revealed weaknesses in the NSA's internal security procedures and the effectiveness of its counterintelligence efforts.

Data analysis played a role in identifying some of the vulnerabilities that Snowden exploited. For example, a review of Snowden's network activity revealed that he had downloaded thousands of files and searched for specific keywords in the months leading up to his departure from the agency. This analysis suggested that Snowden had been planning his actions for some time and had taken steps to cover his tracks.

In addition, a review of the NSA's internal security logs revealed that Snowden had used his administrative privileges to bypass security measures and access files he was not authorized to view. This analysis suggested that the NSA's security protocols were insufficient to prevent an insider from accessing and stealing sensitive information.[18]

In response to the Snowden case, the NSA implemented several changes to its security procedures, including more rigorous background checks for employees and contractors, tighter controls on access to sensitive information, and increased monitoring of network activity. Data analysis supports these significant efforts, as the NSA uses machine learning algorithms to detect anomalous behavior on its networks and identify potential insider threats.

---

[18] For a review of policy changes, see Pohle, J., & Van Audenhove, L. (2017). Post-Snowden internet policy: between public outrage, resistance and policy change. *Media and Communication*, *5*(1), 1–6.

There have been other cases where cybersecurity vulnerabilities have been used for counterespionage.

For instance, in 2018, it was reported that the United States had planted "implants" in Russian power grids as a countermeasure to potential cyberattacks by Russian intelligence services. These implants were essentially pieces of malware that could be activated in the event of an attack, allowing the US to disrupt or disable the power grids.

The implants were reportedly deployed because of intelligence gathered by the NSA, which identified Russian intelligence as having infiltrated US power grids and were capable of causing widespread disruption in the event of a conflict.

While the exact details of the implants and their effectiveness are not publicly known, the case illustrates how cybersecurity vulnerabilities can be used for counterespionage purposes. By identifying vulnerabilities in critical infrastructure systems, such as power grids, and deploying countermeasures to exploit those vulnerabilities, counterintelligence agencies can help prevent or mitigate the impact of cyber espionage attacks.

Summary

Data analysis using advanced algorithms provides unparalleled opportunities to make the most of signals and human intelligence, and to link together entities and events across large graphs. With the global population exceeding 8 billion, and with increased use of electronic communications, creating new algorithms, and finding the available computing power to effectively run those algorithms to produce meaningful reporting and actionable intelligence, remains a challenge for all intelligence agencies.

Chapter 9
Attack Attribution

Attack attribution in counterintelligence refers to the process of identifying the source or perpetrator of a cyber-attack or other malicious activity. In other words, it is the process of determining who is responsible for a particular attack.

Attack attribution can be a challenging task, as attackers often use tactics such as spoofed IP addresses, stolen credentials, and other methods to conceal their identity and location.[1] However, there are several techniques that can be used to attribute an attack, including:

- *Forensic Analysis*: Forensic analysis involves analyzing the digital evidence left behind by an attacker, such as log files, network traffic, and malware samples. This analysis can provide clues about the attacker's identity and location, such as the language used in the malware code or the location of the command-and-control servers.[2]
- *Behavioral Analysis*: Behavioral analysis involves studying the tactics, techniques, and procedures (TTPs) behind an attack. By analyzing the TTPs used in a particular attack, analysts can often identify patterns of behavior that are characteristic of specific threat actors or groups.
- *Open-Source Intelligence*: Open-source intelligence involves gathering information about an attacker from publicly available sources, such as social media profiles, online forums, and other sources. This information can provide clues about the attacker's identity and motivation.[3]

---

[1] For a case study, see Watters, P. A., McCombie, S., Layton, R., & Pieprzyk, J. (2012). Characterising and predicting cyber attacks using the Cyber Attacker Model Profile (CAMP). *Journal of Money Laundering Control*, *15*(4), 430–441.

[2] For a marketplace analysis, see Watters, P. A., & McCombie, S. (2011). A methodology for analyzing the credential marketplace. *Journal of Money Laundering Control*, *14*(1), 32–43.

[3] For an example, see Layton, R., Watters, P., & Dazeley, R. (2012). Recentred local profiles for authorship attribution. *Natural Language Engineering*, *18*(3), 293–312.

P. A. Watters, *Counterintelligence in a Cyber World*,
https://doi.org/10.1007/978-3-031-35287-4_9

- *Collaboration*: Collaboration between different organizations and agencies can also be helpful in attributing an attack. By sharing information and pooling resources, analysts can often build a more complete picture of the attacker and their motivations.

In some cases, attribution can lead to criminal charges and prosecution. For example, 12 Russian military officers in 2018 were indicated because of involvement in hacking the Democratic National Committee during the U.S. presidential election in 2016. The indictment included detailed technical evidence linking the attackers to the Russian military intelligence agency and involved a number of high-tech offenses.[4]

Similarly, in 2017, a Chinese national was arrested and later pleaded guilty to charges related to hacking into U.S. defense contractors' computer systems and stealing sensitive military information. The investigation included extensive technical analysis of the attacker's methods and infrastructure, as well as cooperation between U.S. law enforcement and Chinese authorities.

In summary, attack attribution is an important part of counterintelligence, as it can help organizations to understand who is targeting them and why. By identifying the source of an attack, organizations can take prevention and detection steps as appropriate to the context and scale of the issue.

Forensic Analysis

Digital forensics can be a valuable tool in counterintelligence, as it can help to identify the source of cyber-attacks and other malicious activities. Described below are some ways that digital forensics can be used for counterintelligence:

- *Investigating Cyber Attacks*: Digital forensics can be used to investigate cyberattacks, including malware infections, data breaches, and other types of attacks. By analyzing network traffic, log files, and other tactical data, a picture of the attack vectors can be described.[5]
- *Identifying Insider Threats*: Digital forensics can also be used to identify insider threats, including employees or contractors who may be stealing data or performing other malicious activities. By analyzing activity logs, email records, and other digital evidence, investigators can often identify patterns of behavior that may indicate the presence of an insider threat.

---

[4] For the development of computational linguistic techniques, see Layton, R., McCombie, S., & Watters, P. (2012). Authorship attribution of irc messages using inverse author frequency. In *2012 Third Cybercrime and Trustworthy Computing Workshop* (pp. 7–13). IEEE.

[5] For an example involving network traffic for VOIP, see Azab, A., Watters, P., & Layton, R. (2012, October). Characterising network traffic for skype forensics. In *2012 Third cybercrime and trustworthy computing workshop* (pp. 19–27). IEEE.

- *Data Recovery*: Digital forensics can also be used to recover lost or deleted data, which may be important in investigations or other counterintelligence activities. By using specialized tools and techniques, forensic investigators can often recover data that has been deleted or overwritten.
- *Incident Response*: Digital forensics can be an important part of incident response, as it can help organizations to understand the scope and impact of an incident. By conducting a forensic analysis of the affected systems, investigators can identify the root cause of the incident and develop strategies for preventing future incidents.

In summary, digital forensics can be a powerful tool in counterintelligence, as it provides a way to gather and analyze digital evidence related to cyber-attacks and other malicious activities. By using forensic analysis techniques to investigate incidents and identify patterns of behavior, organizations can develop more effective strategies for preventing and mitigating these threats.

The process of digital forensics involves a range of steps to preserve evidence and show that nothing has been tampered with before it reaches court. The goal is to collect and analyze digital evidence to support or refute a hypothesis related to a crime or an incident.

The following are the key steps involved in producing digital evidence through digital forensics:

- *Acquisition*: The first step in digital forensics is to acquire the digital evidence from the source. This can involve making a copy of a hard drive, collecting network traffic data, or seizing a mobile device. It is important to preserve the chain of evidence to ensure it is admissible in court.
- *Preservation*: Once the digital evidence has been acquired, it must be preserved to prevent any alteration or destruction. This involves creating a secure copy of the original evidence and maintaining a chain of custody to document (or similar).
- *Analysis*: Data is then analyzed to reveal targeted information which can be presented as evidence. This can involve searching for specific files, analyzing system logs, or recovering deleted data.
- *Interpretation*: Once the digital evidence has been analyzed, it must be interpreted to determine its relevance to the case. This involves using technical expertise and knowledge of the case to draw conclusions about the evidence.
- *Presentation*: Finally, the digital evidence must be presented. This involves creating a report that summarizes the findings of the analysis and presenting the evidence in a clear and concise manner.

Digital evidence can focus on many aspects, based on the type of digital device or data that is involved. Here are a few examples of what digital evidence might look like:

- *Digital Images or Videos*: In cases involving images or videos, digital evidence can take the form of digital files such as JPEG, PNG, or MP4. These files can be analyzed to determine the origin of the image or video, any edits that may have been made, and whether the image or video has been manipulated in any way.

- *Computer Files*: In cases involving computer files, digital evidence can take the form of files that have been downloaded or created on a computer or other device. These files may contain important information about a case, such as financial records, emails, or documents.
- *Network Traffic Data*: In cases involving network traffic data, digital evidence can take the form of log files or packet captures that record network activity. These files can be analyzed to identify patterns of behavior or to identify potential sources of a cyber-attack.
- *Social Media Posts*: In cases involving social media activity, digital evidence usually consists of posts, comments, and messages on a range of platforms. These posts can be analyzed to determine who made the post, when it was made, and what was said.
- *Mobile Device Data*: In cases involving mobile devices, digital evidence can take the form of call logs, text messages, photos, and app usage data. This information can be used to establish a timeline of events or to identify potential suspects.

One example of how an attack has been attributed to a group using digital forensics and attribution techniques is the case of WannaCry in the 2017 incident. This attack resulted in many users globally being extorted.

After the attack, several cybersecurity firms conducted forensic analyses of the malware and its behavior, and identified several characteristics that suggested the attack was carried out by Lazarus, believed to originate from North Korea, and state-sposnored. Lazarus was also behind the highly publicised 2014 Sony Pictures hack.[6]

Some of the key attribution factors that led cybersecurity firms to identify Lazarus as the group behind the WannaCry attack included:

- *Code similarities*: The WannaCry malware contained code that was like code used in previous attacks attributed to Lazarus.
- *Command and control infrastructure*: The malware used command and control infrastructure that had been previously used by Lazarus.
- *Motivation*: The ransomware attack was seen as an unusual tactic for a hacking group, and it was speculated that Lazarus may have been motivated by financial gain.
- *Political context*: The attack coincided with rising tensions between North Korea and the United States and was seen as a possible retaliation for increased sanctions and other measures taken against North Korea.

In technical terms, the Lazarus command and control (C&C) structure is a critical part of its operations, as it allows the group to control infected computers and exfiltrate stolen data.

---

[6] For an overview, see Haggard, S., & Lindsay, J. R. (2015). North Korea and the Sony hack: Exporting instability through cyberspace.

Described below are some of the key characteristics of Lazarus' command and control structure:

- *Use of proxies*: Lazarus typically uses a network of proxies to communicate with infected computers and hide the location of its command-and-control servers. These proxies are often geographically dispersed, making it difficult for investigators to trace the group's activities.
- *Encrypted communications*: Lazarus uses sophisticated encryption techniques to communicate with infected computers and exfiltrate stolen information, presenting a challenge for interception of the group's communications.
- *Infrastructure reuse*: Lazarus often reuses command and control infrastructure in multiple attacks, making it easier for investigators to link different attacks to the same group.
- *Custom malware*: Lazarus uses custom malware that is tailored to specific targets and designed to evade detection by security software. This malware is often delivered through phishing emails or other social engineering tactics.

In summary, the command-and-control structure used by Lazarus is designed to enable the group to carry out attacks while avoiding detection and attribution. By using a network of proxies, encryption techniques, and custom malware, the group can control infected computers, exfiltrate data, and carry out attacks on a global scale.[7] The attribution techniques used by cybersecurity firms in the case of the WannaCry attack provided a strong case for the involvement of Lazarus and helped to inform responses and countermeasures against future attacks.

Behavioral Analysis

Behavioral analysis in counterintelligence involves monitoring and analyzing the behavior of individuals or groups to find threats or suggest potential vulnerabilities. Described below are some of the key elements of how behavioral analysis works in counterintelligence:

- *Collection of data*: Behavioral analysis relies on source information from a range of origins, including open-source intelligence, social media activity, financial records, travel patterns, and other sources of information. This data is often collected through automated tools but may also be gathered through human intelligence sources.
- *Analysis of behavior patterns*: Once data has been collected, analysts use a variety of tools and techniques to identify patterns in behavior that may indicate a

---

[7] For a technical analysis, see Ahn, G., Lee, S. A., & Park, W. H. (2021). Changes of Cyber Hacking Attack Aspect of North Korea Cyber-Attack Groups Applying MITRE ATT&CK. *Research Briefs on Information and Communication Technology Evolution, 7*, 75–88.

threat. These patterns may include changes in communication patterns, travel habits, financial transactions, or other indicators of suspicious activity.

- *Development of profiles*: Based on the analysis of behavior patterns, analysts may develop profiles of individuals or groups that are of interest to counterintelligence efforts. These profiles may include information about the individual's background, affiliations, motivations, and potential vulnerabilities.
- *Identification of anomalies*: Behavioral analysis also involves the identification of anomalies that may indicate a potential threat or vulnerability. These anomalies may include sudden changes in behavior patterns, unusual financial transactions, or other indicators of suspicious activity.
- *Risk assessments*: Finally, behavioral analysis is used to assess the level of risk posed by individuals or groups of interest. This may involve evaluating the potential impact of a threat, the likelihood of an attack or other malicious activity, and the effectiveness of countermeasures.

In summary, behavioral analysis is an important part of counterintelligence efforts, as it provides a way to identify potential threats and vulnerabilities by monitoring and analyzing patterns of behavior. By developing profiles of individuals or groups of interest and assessing the level of risk posed by these entities, counterintelligence organizations can develop more effective strategies for mitigating threats and protecting national security.

Anomaly detection can be used to attribute activity to a malicious individual or group, such as what occurred in the Silk Road case. The perpetrator – Ross Ulbricht - was charged with a range of crimes, including drug trafficking, money laundering, and computer hacking.[8]

During the investigation, the FBI analyzed data from the Silk Road website and identified several anomalies that indicated Ulbricht was the mastermind behind the operation. For example, they found evidence that Ulbricht had used the same username, "Dread Pirate Roberts," on both Silk Road and other websites where he had discussed his involvement in the marketplace.

The FBI also discovered that Ulbricht had used a public Wi-Fi network at a San Francisco library to access the Silk Road website and make changes to the site's code. By analyzing the Wi-Fi data, the FBI was able to link Ulbricht to the library's IP address and use this as evidence in his trial.

The evidence used in the case can be summarized as follows:

- *Digital forensics*: During the investigation, the FBI seized Ulbricht's laptop and conducted a digital forensic analysis of the device. They found evidence that Ulbricht ran Silk Road, including chat logs and email correspondence that linked Ulbricht to the Dread Pirate Roberts username used on the site.

---

[8] For a user perspective, see Van Hout, M. C., & Bingham, T. (2013). 'Silk Road', the virtual drug marketplace: A single case study of user experiences. *International Journal of Drug Policy*, 24(5), 385–391.

- *Online activities*: The FBI also analyzed Ulbricht's online activities and found evidence that he had posted about his involvement in the Silk Road on various forums and social media platforms using the same username.
- *Bitcoin transactions*: The Silk Road relied on the use of the cryptocurrency Bitcoin for transactions, and the FBI analyzed Bitcoin transactions to track the flow of money on the site. They were able to link these transactions to Ulbricht's personal accounts, providing further evidence of his involvement in the operation.
- *Surveillance footage*: The FBI also obtained surveillance footage from the San Francisco library where he accessed the website. Footage showed Ulbricht using a laptop while the target account was logged in to the site, providing strong evidence that Ulbricht was the person behind the account.
- *Witness testimony*: Finally, the prosecution called several witnesses to testify against Ulbricht, including former Silk Road employees who had worked with him directly and provided testimony about his involvement in the site's operations.

Ultimately, these anomalies in the internet data helped prosecutors secure a conviction against Ulbricht.

On a side note, it is very instructive to review the role that Bitcoin transactions played in securing a conviction. Bitcoin transactions can be used as digital evidence in a few ways, including:

- *Tracking the flow of money*: Bitcoin transactions are recorded on a public ledger called the blockchain, which allows investigators to trace the movement of funds between different Bitcoin addresses. By analyzing these transactions, investigators can identify patterns of behavior and track the flow of money to and from specific individuals or organizations.
- *Linking transactions to specific individuals*: Although Bitcoin transactions are anonymous, they are also recorded on the blockchain, which makes it possible to link transactions to specific individuals or addresses.[9] Investigators can use this information to identify suspects and build a case against them.
- *Identifying patterns of behavior*: Bitcoin transactions can also be used to identify patterns of behavior that may be indicative of criminal activity. For example, investigators may look for transactions that are consistent with money laundering, such as financial transfers across multiple Bitcoin addresses in a short period of time.
- *Corroborating other evidence*: Bitcoin transactions can also be used to corroborate other forms of evidence, such as digital forensics or witness testimony. For example, if investigators find evidence on a suspect's computer that links them to a specific Bitcoin address, they may be able to use transaction records to confirm that the suspect was involved in the transactions associated with that address.

---

[9] For a review of vulnerabilities, see Alkhalifah, A., Ng, A., Kayes, A. S. M., Chowdhury, J., Alazab, M., & Watters, P. A. (2020). A taxonomy of blockchain threats and vulnerabilities. In *Blockchain for Cybersecurity and Privacy* (pp. 3–28). CRC Press.

This case demonstrates how the analysis of internet data can be used to identify anomalies that can be indicative of criminal activity. By analyzing patterns of behavior and linking online activities to specific individuals, law enforcement agencies can build a strong case against individuals who engage in illegal activities online.

Open-Source Intelligence

Attributing cyber-attacks using open source intelligence (OSINT) can be a challenging task, as cyber criminals often use a variety of methods to conceal their identity and location. However, OSINT can still be a useful tool for identifying the origin and perpetrator of a cyber-attack. Described below are some steps that can be taken to attribute cyber-attacks using OSINT:

- *Gather and analyze technical data*: Analyze technical data such as network traffic logs, system event logs, and malware samples. These IOCs can be used to identify the tools and techniques used by the attacker.
- *Authorship Analysis*: Use supervised and unsupervised learning techniques to try to recover (or at least link) identities based on pseudonyms via linguistic analysis,[10] including short texts such as Twitter.[11]
- *Analyze social media and online forums*: Analyze social media platforms and online forums to look for clues that might help identify the attacker.[12] For example, attackers may brag about their exploits on forums or social media platforms, or they may accidentally reveal information about themselves in their posts.
- *Investigate domain registration information*: Investigate domain registration information to identify the individual or organization that registered a particular domain name. This information can be used to identify the owner of the domain, which could be the attacker.
- *Analyze malware code*: Analyze the code of malware used in the attack to identify unique characteristics or patterns that could be used to link the attack to a particular group or individual.
- *Monitor the dark web*: Monitor the dark web for any communications or transactions related to the attack. This could include the sale of stolen data or tools used in the attack.

---

[10] For an outline, see Layton, R., Watters, P. A., & Dazeley, R. (2015). Authorship analysis of aliases: Does topic influence accuracy?. *Natural Language Engineering*, *21*(4), 497–518.

[11] For an example, see Layton, R., Watters, P., & Dazeley, R. (2010, July). Authorship attribution for twitter in 140 characters or less. In *2010 Second Cybercrime and Trustworthy Computing Workshop* (pp. 1–8). IEEE.

[12] The range of clues could include fake or false flag data, for an example, see Layton, R., Watters, P., & Ureche, O. (2013, November). Identifying faked hotel reviews using authorship analysis. In *2013 Fourth Cybercrime and Trustworthy Computing Workshop* (pp. 1–6). IEEE.

- *Collaborate with law enforcement*: Work with law enforcement agencies to share information and resources that could help identify the attacker. This could include sharing technical data or collaborating on investigations.

Several cases have used domain registration information for counterintelligence purposes. One example is the case of Operation Ghost Click, which was a large-scale cybercriminal operation that was taken down by the FBI in 2011.[13]

The operation involved a group of cybercriminals who used malware to redirect their internet traffic to websites that they controlled. This allowed them to generate fraudulent advertising revenue, earning them millions of dollars.

During the investigation, the FBI was able to identify the individuals behind the operation by analyzing domain registration information. Especially, they were able to trace the ownership of the domains used in the operation to a company called Rove Digital, which was based in Estonia.

Further investigation revealed that the owners of Rove Digital were a group of six Estonian nationals who had set up the company as a front for their criminal activities. The FBI worked with Estonian law enforcement agencies to arrest the individuals and dismantle the operation.

Domain registration data misused in this case highlights the importance of OSINT in counterintelligence operations. By analyzing publicly available information, investigators were able to identify the individuals behind a sophisticated cybercriminal operation and bring them to justice. However, using this type of data is harder than it first seems for a few reasons. ICANN, the Internet Corporation for Assigned Names and Numbers, runs the domain name system (DNS), ensuring that domain names are allocated and registered correctly. One of the policy issues that ICANN faces in relation to the validity of domain name data is the accuracy and reliability of the domain name registration data. Described below are some of the key policy issues that ICANN faces:

- *Verification of domain name registrant data*: ICANN requires domain name registrars to collect proper and valid data about registrants behind a domain name, including their name, address, and contact information. However, there are concerns that some registrars may not be verifying this information properly, which could lead to the registration of domains with inaccurate or false information.
- *Privacy and data protection*: ICANN has faced criticism for requiring registrars to collect personal information about domain name registrants, which some argue could infringe on privacy rights. There are ongoing debates about how to balance the need for accurate registration data with the need to protect individual privacy.[14]

---

[13] For analysis, see Alrwais, S. A., Gerber, A., Dunn, C. W., Spatscheck, O., Gupta, M., & Osterweil, E. (2012, December). Dissecting ghost clicks: Ad fraud via misdirected human clicks. In *Proceedings of the 28th Annual Computer Security Applications Conference* (pp. 21–30).

[14] For a Chinese case study, see Comb, M., & Watters, P. A. (2016, December). Peeking behind the great firewall: Privacy on Chinese file sharing networks. In *2016 14th Annual Conference on Privacy, Security and Trust (PST)* (pp. 650–656). IEEE.

- *Enforcement of accuracy requirements*: ICANN has established rules and policies around the accuracy of domain name registration data, but there are concerns about how these requirements are enforced. Some argue that ICANN should be proactive in imposing sanctions on registrars that fail to comply with the rules, but – you guessed it – this rarely happens.
- *International cooperation*: Domain name registration data is often subject to different legal requirements and standards in different jurisdictions, which can make it difficult to provide assurance around reliability. ICANN faces the challenge of working with stakeholders in different countries to establish consistent policies and standards for domain name registration data.

In summary, ensuring the validity of domain name data is an important policy issue for ICANN, as inaccurate or false registration data can have serious consequences for the security and stability of the DNS.[15] ICANN must continue to work with stakeholders to address these issues and establish policies and standards that promote accurate and reliable domain name registration data.

As mentioned above, authorship analysis is another field of study that uses linguistic and behavioral characteristics for authorship communication style identification, even where pseudonyms are used, or anonymization has been performed. In some cases, authorship analysis can be used to recover the anonymous identities of individuals who have attempted to conceal their identity. Described below are some of the ways in which authorship analysis can be used for this purpose:

- *Linguistic analysis*: Used to distinguish linguistic patterns that are unique to an individual. By analyzing the language used in a text or communication, researchers can identify patterns of grammar, vocabulary, and writing style that can be used to identify the author.[16]
- *Behavioral analysis*: Authorship analysis can also be used to identify behavioral patterns that are unique to an individual. For example, researchers can analyze the timing and frequency of communications to identify patterns of behavior that are consistent with a particular individual.
- *Contextual analysis*: Authorship analysis can also involve analyzing the context in which a communication was made. For example, researchers may analyze metadata associated with a text or communication, such as the date and time it was sent or the device it was sent from, to identify patterns that can help identify the author.[17]

---

[15] For a review, see Watters, P. A., Herps, A., Layton, R., & McCombie, S. (2013). ICANN or ICANT: Is WHOIS an Enabler of Cybercrime?. In *2013 Fourth Cybercrime and Trustworthy Computing Workshop* (pp. 44–49). IEEE.

[16] For a novel algorithm, see Layton, R., Watters, P., & Dazeley, R. (2013). Evaluating authorship distance methods using the positive Silhouette coefficient. *Natural Language Engineering, 19*(4), 517–535.

[17] For a case study, see Layton, R., Watters, P., & Dazeley, R. (2013). Local n-grams for Author Identification. *Notebook for PAN at CLEF.*

- *AI*: AI techniques can be used to identify patterns in large datasets that would be difficult to detect through manual analysis. These techniques can help researchers identify linguistic and behavioral patterns that are unique to an individual.

Both supervised and unsupervised authorship analysis have been applied to counterintelligence problems. Supervised authorship analysis is a type of authorship attribution that involves using a known set of texts from different authors to train a statistical model, to classify or identify the authorship of unknown or disputed texts. Described below are some key characteristics of supervised authorship analysis:

- *Training data*: The method relies on a set of known texts from different authors, which are used to train the algorithm or model. These texts are carefully selected to be representative of each author's unique writing style.
- *Feature selection*: The algorithm or model relies on specific linguistic features to identify the authorship of a text. These features may include word choice, sentence structure, punctuation, and other linguistic markers.
- *Statistical analysis*: The algorithm or model uses statistical analysis to estimate the likelihood that a particular text was written by a specific individual, based on the identified features.
- *Machine learning*: In many cases, supervised authorship analysis relies on machine learning algorithms, which can learn to identify patterns and relationships between the features and the known authors and use this information to make predictions about the authorship of unknown texts.
- *Accuracy and error rates*: The accuracy of supervised algorithms relies on the training data quality, the characteristics selected, plus the algorithm or model used. Like any machine learning approach, there is a risk of overfitting, which can result in high error rates and poor generalization to new data.
- *Legal admissibility*: Supervised authorship analysis is increasingly being used in legal contexts, such as plagiarism cases or criminal investigations. As with any forensic evidence, it must meet certain legal standards for reliability, validity, and admissibility.

In contrast, unsupervised authorship analysis is a type of authorship attribution that does not rely on a pre-defined set of known authors or training data. Instead, it uses statistical methods or machine learning algorithms to identify patterns and clusters, and then uses these patterns to group texts into clusters that are likely to have been written by the same author. Described below are some key characteristics of unsupervised authorship analysis:

- *Lack of training data*: Unlike supervised authorship analysis, unsupervised authorship analysis does not require a pre-defined set of texts from known authors. Instead, it relies on a large corpus of texts, such as a collection of emails, social media posts, or blog articles.
- *Feature selection*: The algorithm or model identifies the most important linguistic features in the corpus, based on their frequency, variance, or other statistical properties. These features may include word choice, sentence structure, punctuation, and other linguistic markers.

- *Clustering*: The algorithm or model uses a range of techniques to group texts into clusters based on the identified features. The number and size of clusters is determined automatically by the algorithm, without any prior knowledge of the authors.
- *Accuracy and reliability*: Unsupervised authorship analysis can be more challenging than supervised analysis, as there is no ground truth or known authors to compare the results to. The accuracy and reliability may vary considerably.
- *Scalability*: Unsupervised authorship analysis is highly scalable, as it can be applied to very large datasets and does not require manual labeling or annotation of texts.
- *Interpretability*: Unsupervised authorship analysis can be less interpretable than supervised analysis, as it may not provide clear evidence of specific linguistic features or patterns that are associated with specific authors.

Below is an example of how unsupervised authorship analysis could be used in the context of counterintelligence:

Suppose a security agency has intercepted a large corpus of emails exchanged between suspected foreign agents and their handlers. The agency suspects that the agents are using coded language and pseudonyms to communicate and wants to identify the different groups of agents and handlers based on their writing style and linguistic patterns.

Here are the steps that could be taken for unsupervised authorship analysis:

- *Preprocessing*: The text data is preprocessed to remove any noise or irrelevant information, such as metadata, headers, footers, and signatures. The text is then tokenized into words and normalized by removing stop words, punctuation, and capitalization.
- *Feature selection*: The most relevant linguistic features are selected based on their frequency and variance in the corpus. For example, features such as word frequency, sentence length, use of punctuation, and use of specific keywords or phrases may be selected.
- *Clustering*: The selected features are used to cluster the emails into groups using an appropriate algorithm, with parameters selected by analyzing the within-cluster sum of squares (WSS) or silhouette scores, or by using elbow or silhouette plots to visualize the optimal number of clusters.
- *Interpretation*: The resulting clusters are analyzed to identify the different groups of agents and handlers based on their writing style and linguistic patterns. For example, certain clusters may be identified as using more complex sentence structures or coded language, while others may be identified as using simpler language or more direct communication. These clusters can be further analyzed to identify potential patterns of behavior or communication that can inform counterintelligence operations.

One limitation of unsupervised authorship analysis is that it may not provide conclusive evidence of specific authors or groups and may require additional analysis or investigation to confirm suspicions or identify specific individuals. However, it can be a useful tool for identifying patterns and clusters of linguistic features that can inform counterintelligence efforts.

Authorship analysis has been used in some high-profile cases for prosecution purposes. One such example is the case of the Unabomber, Theodore Kaczynski. In this case, linguistic analysis was used to identify Kaczynski as the author of the Unabomber Manifesto, a document that was sent to several newspapers and contained the Unabomber's political and social beliefs. The analysis focused on the linguistic patterns and vocabulary used in the manifesto and compared it to Kaczynski's other writings, ultimately leading to his identification and capture.

Another example is the case of the BTK (Bind, Torture, Kill) serial killer, Dennis Rader.[18] In this case, authorship analysis was used to connect Rader to several letters and messages that were sent to police and media outlets, including a message that was left in a book at a public library. The analysis focused on the language, syntax, and writing style of the letters and compared them to Rader's personal writings, ultimately leading to his arrest and conviction.

In the UK, authorship analysis was used to identify a British man who was posting propaganda for the Islamic State on social media. The analysis focused on the language, syntax, and writing style used in the propaganda and compared it to the man's personal writings, ultimately leading to his identification and prosecution under terrorism-related charges.[19]

These examples demonstrate the potential of authorship analysis in forensic investigations and prosecutions, but this approach may be just one among many and should be used in conjunction with other investigative techniques and evidence. Additionally, the accuracy rests upon the quality and quantity of the available texts and the skill and expertise of the analysts performing the analysis.

In summary, authorship analysis can be a powerful tool for recovering anonymous identities, but it requires knowledge of linguistic and behavioral patterns, plus access to large datasets and sophisticated analytical tools. In addition, there are ethical and legal considerations around the use of authorship analysis to identify individuals, and it is important to consider these factors when conducting this type of analysis.

Summary

Combining OSINT with digital forensics is a potent defensive tool. However, it is significant to note that attributing cyber-attacks using OSINT is not always straightforward and may need a lot of time and effort. In addition, attribution can never be 100% certain, as hackers may use various approaches to hide their true identity and geographic position.

---

[18] For a case study, see Williams, N. D., & Landwehr, K. (2006). Bind, torture, kill: The BTK investigation. *Police Chief, 73*(12), 16.

[19] For an overview, see Macnair, L., & Frank, R. (2017). "To My Brothers in the West...": A Thematic Analysis of Videos Produced by the Islamic State's al-Hayat Media Center. *Journal of contemporary criminal justice, 33*(3), 234–253.

Chapter 10
Practical Deception

Deception can be a useful tool for counterintelligence operations because it allows intelligence agencies to mislead adversaries and disrupt their activities. Described below are some ways in which deception can be used for counterintelligence:

- *Disinformation*: Disinformation involves intentionally spreading false or misleading information to an adversary to confuse or mislead them. This can be done through direct interactions. By spreading disinformation, intelligence agencies can disrupt adversary operations and sow confusion among their ranks.
- *False flag operations*: False flag operations involve conducting an operation in such a way that it appears to be the work of another party. For example, an intelligence agency might carry out a cyber-attack and make it appear as if it was conducted by a different country or group. False flag operations can be used to attribute blame to another party or to create confusion and mistrust among adversaries.
- *Agent provocateurs*: An agent provocateur is a person who is recruited by an intelligence agency to act as a provocateur in a target organization. By posing as a member of the target organization, the agent can gain the trust of other members and potentially influence their actions. This technique can be used to disrupt adversary activities and gather intelligence.
- *Feeding misinformation*: Feeding misinformation involves intentionally providing untrue data to an adversary to sway their actions. For example, an intelligence agency might provide false information about the location of a target or the capabilities of their own forces to influence an adversary's decision-making process.
- *Honeypots*: A honeypot is a security mechanism that is designed to look like a vulnerable system or network to attract attackers. Once an attacker has accessed

© The Author(s), under exclusive license to Springer Nature Switzerland AG 2023   111
P. A. Watters, *Counterintelligence in a Cyber World*,
https://doi.org/10.1007/978-3-031-35287-4_10

the honeypot, they can be monitored, and their actions can be analyzed for intelligence purposes[1]

Anna Chapman is a case in hand, from 2010. Chapman and her fellow Russian spies were accused of using false identities, deception, and covert communication techniques to gather information and pass it on to the Russian government. Chapman had a cover identity as a successful entrepreneur and used her charm and networking skills to gain access to influential circles in the US.

In summary, deception can be a powerful tool for counterintelligence, but it requires careful planning and execution. Deception operations must be designed in a way that minimizes the risk of detection and avoids unintended consequences. In addition, there are ethical and legal considerations around the use of deception in intelligence operations, and it is important to consider these factors when conducting this type of activity.

Honeypots and Honeynets

Honeypots can be used for deception in several ways:

- *Attracting attackers*: By setting up a honeypot that appears to be a vulnerable system or network, intelligence agencies can attract attackers and gain insight into their tactics and techniques.
- *Gathering intelligence*: Once an attacker has accessed a honeypot, their actions can be monitored and analyzed for intelligence purposes. For example, analysts can focus on the attacker's geographic position, their methods of attack, and their objectives.[2]
- *Misleading attackers*: By using honeypots, intelligence agencies can mislead attackers and disrupt their activities. For example, a honeypot might be set up to appear as a high-value target, only to lead the attacker to a dead end or to expose them to countermeasures.
- *Testing and evaluating defenses*: Honeypots can also be used to test and evaluate an organization's defenses against cyber-attacks. By simulating real-world attacks, honeypots can help organizations identify vulnerabilities and weaknesses in their security posture.

Honeypots can support deception in cybersecurity and counterintelligence. However, like any deception operation, honeypots must be carefully planned and executed to minimize the risk of unintended consequences. In addition,

---

[1] For a review, see Scanlan, J., Watters, P. A., Prichard, J., Hunn, C., Spiranovic, C., & Wortley, R. (2022). Creating honeypots to prevent online child exploitation. *Future Internet*, *14*(4), 121.

[2] For examples, see Prichard, J., Krone, T., Spiranovic, C., & Watters, P. (2018). Transdisciplinary research in virtual space: can online warning messages reduce engagement with child exploitation material?. In *Routledge handbook of crime science* (pp. 309–319). Routledge.

organizations must ensure that they have the appropriate legal and ethical authorization before deploying honeypots.

In the early 2000s, security researcher Lance Spitzner created a honeypot called "Honeynet" to study the behavior of hackers and malware. Honeynet was designed to look like a real corporate network, complete with fake employee names, email accounts, and network services. The system was set up with intentionally weak security controls to attract hackers.[3]

Over the course of several weeks, attackers from around the world began to probe the Honeynet system, attempting to gain access and exploit vulnerabilities. Spitzner and his team monitored the attackers' activities and collected data on their methods and tactics. They were able to identify several new and previously unknown malware samples, as well as gain insight into the tactics and techniques used by attackers.

One noteworthy finding from the Honeynet project was the discovery of a new type of worm called "Agobot". The worm was able to evade traditional antivirus software and spread quickly through networks, causing significant damage. Thanks to the Honeynet project, security researchers were able to study Agobot and develop new methods for detecting and mitigating its effects.[4]

In summary, the Honeynet project demonstrated the value of honeypots as a tool for studying the behavior of attackers and developing new methods for defending against cyber-attacks. Since then, honeypots have become a widely used tool in cybersecurity research and defense.

Another example of honeypot usage has been used to study the behavior of individuals who engage in the distribution of child sexual abuse material (CSAM) online.[5] These honeypots are designed to mimic websites, forums, or peer-to-peer networks where CSAM is shared, with the goal of attracting individuals who are actively seeking or distributing CSAM.

The use of CSAM honeypots is a controversial technique, as it involves the creation of apparently illegal content to lure individuals who are engaging in illegal activity. However, proponents of the technique argue that it can be a useful tool for identifying and prosecuting individuals who are engaged in the distribution of CSAM.

One noteworthy example of the use of CSAM honeypots is the "HoneyNet Project" by the German police. This project involved the creation of a fake website that appeared to be a forum for sharing CSAM. The police were able to identify a few individuals who visited the site and engaged in illegal activity, leading to arrests and prosecutions.

---

[3] Read the original! For details, see Spitzner, L. (2003). The honeynet project: Trapping the hackers. *IEEE Security & Privacy, 1*(2), 15–23.

[4] For details, see McLaughlin, L. (2004). Bot software spreads, causes new worries. *IEEE Distributed Systems Online, 5*(6), 1.

[5] For a review, see Prichard, J., Scanlan, J., Krone, T., Spiranovic, C., Watters, P., & Wortley, R. (2022). Warning messages to prevent illegal sharing of sexual images: Results of a randomised controlled experiment. *Trends and Issues in Crime and Criminal Justice.*

Another example is the "Project Vic" initiative by the NCMEC in the United States. Project Vic involves the creation of a database of known CSAM images and the use of CSAM honeypots to identify new images and track their distribution.[6]

A final example involved the recruitment of naïve participants using a bodybuilding site through advertising. The study integrated real and fake advertising networks, on which a few fake CSAM sites were apparently advertising. The honeypot was used to experimentally determine – for the first time – which deterrence approaches might be effective, when compared to a control condition. The evidence gathered has been used to develop and evaluate policy and has fed into a broader program work involving chatbots and other mechanisms to engage potential offenders.[7]

In summary, a honeypot be a useful tool for identifying and prosecuting individuals who are engaged in the distribution of CSAM, and that its potential benefits may outweigh the risks.

Disinformation and Misinformation

Disinformation is fake data propagated intentionally to achieve widespread deception, such as videos, manipulated social media posts, and propaganda. The purpose of disinformation is often to sow confusion, create distrust, and manipulate public opinion.

Disinformation is often spread by individuals or organizations with a political or ideological agenda, but it can also be spread for financial gain or simply for the sake of causing chaos. In recent years, the spread of disinformation has become a major concern, particularly in election campaigns and a range of social and digital media.

One key feature of disinformation is that it often contains a kernel of truth, which can make it difficult to distinguish from accurate information. Disinformation can be disseminated using all of the major technology and communications channels available today.

Disinformation can have a broad social impact, such as influencing the outcome of elections, inciting violence, and eroding trust in institutions. In response, many organizations and governments are working to develop strategies to combat disinformation, such as fact-checking, media literacy programs, and efforts to promote greater transparency and accountability in online communication.

Misinformation, in contrast, is untrue or inaccurate information that is spread unintentionally and without malicious intentions. Unlike disinformation, which is

---

[6] For details, see Acar, K. V. (2020). Framework for a single global repository of child abuse materials. *Global Policy, 11*(1), 178–190.

[7] For a literature survey, see Prichard, J., Scanlan, J. D., Watters, P., Wortley, R., Hunn, C., & Garrett, E. P. (2022). Online messages to reduce users' engagement with child sexual abuse material: a review of relevant literature for the reThink chatbot.

deliberately created and spread to deceive people, misinformation can result from a variety of factors, including errors, misunderstandings, and honest mistakes.

Misinformation may include fairly obscure forms, such as urban legends. It can also be spread through various channels, including word of mouth, social media, and news outlets. Misinformation can be particularly widespread and persistent in situations where accurate information is scarce or difficult to obtain, such as during emergencies or natural disasters.

The spread of misinformation can have serious consequences, such as contributing to public panic or confusion, undermining trust in institutions, and even causing harm to individuals or communities. In recent years, the spread of misinformation has become a major concern, particularly in the context of social media, where false or misleading information can quickly go viral and reach a large audience.

Efforts to combat misinformation include fact-checking, media literacy programs, and efforts to promote greater transparency and accountability in online communication. However, because misinformation can be difficult to identify and correct, it remains a persistent challenge for individuals, organizations, and governments alike.

One example of how disinformation has the potential to undermine democracy is Donald Trump's 2016 election campaign. This campaign allegedly involved disinformation dissemination at a large scale, as well as targeted advertising and other tactics.[8]

One key aspect of the disinformation campaign was the use of false news stories and propaganda, which were designed to manipulate public opinion and sow confusion. These false stories were often spread through social media and other online channels, where they could reach a large audience quickly and easily.

Another aspect of the campaign was utilization of automated accounts to spread untruths and amplify false narratives, also knowns as "bots". These accounts were often used to artificially inflate the reach and influence of false stories, making them appear more popular and authoritative than they were.

The impact of the disinformation campaign on the election is difficult to quantify, but many experts believe that it had a significant impact on the outcome. By manipulating public opinion and sowing confusion, the campaign may have helped to influence the election outcome, who won by a narrow margin in several key states.

This case study demonstrates the complexity of information operations and how they can potentially undermine democracy by manipulating public opinion and distorting the truth.[9]

In the context of national security, misinformation can be used to protect sensitive information, operations, and personnel from hostile actors. This can involve intentionally planting false information or misleading narratives to mislead or confuse adversaries.

---

[8] For analysis, see Walter, N., Cohen, J., Holbert, R. L., & Morag, Y. (2020). Fact-checking: A meta-analysis of what works and for whom. *Political Communication*, *37*(3), 350–375.

[9] For a review, see Allcott, H., & Gentzkow, M. (2017). Social media and fake news in the 2016 election. *Journal of economic perspectives*, *31*(2), 211–236.

One instance of how misinformation has been used in national security deception. Military deception involves the use of misleading information or actions to mislead adversaries and shape their perceptions of military capabilities, intentions, or activities. For example, a military organization might intentionally leak false information or conduct deceptive activities to mislead an adversary about the location or capabilities of military forces. This can help to misdirect the adversary's attention and resources and increase the chances of success in military operations.

Another example of how misinformation has been used in national security is in the context of intelligence operations. Intelligence agencies might intentionally plant false information or stories to mislead or confuse foreign intelligence services or other hostile actors. For example, a foreign intelligence service might be fed false information about the capabilities or intentions of a military organization, to mislead them about the true nature of the organization's activities, protecting classified information or operations and increase the chances of success in intelligence operations.

Finally – and perhaps the most relevant to the current decade – was the plethora of COVID misinformation. During the COVID-19 pandemic, misinformation and false claims about the virus and vaccines have been widely circulated on social media platforms. One example of this is the claim that COVID-19 vaccines are dangerous and can cause infertility in women. Automated tools to measure attitudes to these phenomena have been developed.[10]

This claim originated from a blog post that was widely shared on social media, despite being based on a misinterpretation of a study that had nothing to do with COVID-19 vaccines. The claim gained further traction when it was promoted by anti-vaccine groups and individuals on social media.

To combat this misinformation, researchers at the University of Alberta in Canada conducted a study using machine learning to identify and analyze tweets related to COVID-19 vaccines and infertility. They collected a dataset of tweets containing relevant keywords and used natural language processing and sentiment analysis techniques to identify tweets containing misinformation and false claims.[11]

The researchers found that a significant proportion of the tweets containing the claim about COVID-19 vaccines and infertility were being shared by accounts with a history of promoting conspiracy theories and misinformation about vaccines. They also found that these accounts were using a variety of tactics to spread their message, including the use of hashtags and the amplification of content through retweets and replies.

The study highlights the importance of using a range of algorithms to monitor and combat the spread of misinformation about COVID-19 and other public health

---

[10] For an example, see Kayes, A. S. M., Islam, M. S., Watters, P. A., Ng, A., & Kayesh, H. (2020). Automated measurement of attitudes towards social distancing using social media: a COVID-19 case study.

[11] For more examples, see Evanega, S., Lynas, M., Adams, J., Smolenyak, K., & Insights, C. G. (2020). Coronavirus misinformation: quantifying sources and themes in the COVID-19 'infodemic'. *JMIR Preprints, 19*(10), 2020.

issues on social media platforms. By identifying and analyzing the sources and tactics used to spread misinformation, researchers and public health officials can develop targeted strategies to counter the spread of false information and promote accurate and reliable information to the public.[12]

False Flag Operations

These attacks are carried out by a government or other organization, in which the operation is designed to appear as though it was carried out by a different group or country. The purpose of a false flag operation is often to deceive or mislead other countries or groups, or to justify a military or political response.

False flag operations can take many forms. For example, a government might carry out a terrorist attack and make it appear as though it was carried out by a different group, to justify military action against that group. Alternatively, a government might stage an incident, such as a border skirmish or a naval blockade, and make it appear as though it was provoked by another country, to justify a military response.

False flag operations have been used throughout history, and are often associated with espionage, covert action, and military deception. However, false flag operations are generally considered to be unethical and illegal. In some cases, the use of false flag operations can lead to diplomatic or military conflict or erode trust and cooperation between countries.

In the context of cybersecurity, a false flag operation involves an attacker disguising their identity or location to make it appear as though the attack was carried out by a different group or country. The goal of a cyber false flag operation is often to mislead investigators, deflect blame, or create a justification for retaliatory action.

A cyber false flag operation may be effected tactically in a range of different actions. For example, an attacker might use a virtual private network (VPN) or a proxy server to hide their true IP address and location. This can make it more difficult for investigators to trace the attack back to the attacker.

Another technique that attackers might use is to use malware or other tools that are associated with a different group or country. For example, an attacker might use a malware tool that is commonly used by a known threat group, to make it appear as though the attack was carried out by that group.[13]

In some cases, attackers might even go so far as to leave false clues or deliberately misleading evidence, to further confuse investigators and deflect blame.

---

[12] For a review of sentiment analysis, see Prichard, J., Watters, P., Krone, T., Spiranovic, C., & Cockburn, H. (2015). Social media sentiment analysis: A new empirical tool for assessing public opinion on crime?. *Current Issues in Criminal Justice*, 27(2), 217–236.

[13] For a case study, see Layton, R., & Watters, P. A. (2014). A methodology for estimating the tangible cost of data breaches. *Journal of Information Security and Applications*, 19(6), 321–330.

False flag operations in the cyber context can be particularly difficult to detect and attribute, as attackers can easily hide their identity and location using a variety of tools and techniques. As such, it is important for investigators and analysts to carefully examine all available evidence and consider multiple hypotheses when attempting to attribute a cyber-attack.

One case study in recent times involved the use of a VPN occurred in 2017, when a group of attackers used a VPN to attack a Saudi Arabian petrochemical plant.[14]

A VPN, or Virtual Private Network, is a technology that allows users to create a secure and private network connection over the internet. When a user connects to a VPN, their data is encrypted and sent via a remote server, which can be located anywhere in the world. This can make it more difficult for others to monitor or intercept the user's internet activity and can also allow the user to bypass geographic restrictions or censorship.[15]

In the context of a false flag operation, a VPN can be used to disguise the true location of the attacker and make it appear as though the attack is coming from a different country or region. This can make it more difficult for investigators to attribute data to an actual source and may help the attacker to evade detection or attribution.

In the context of this attack, which was at first attributed to a new threat group known as "Greenbug," was eventually discovered to be the work of a different group, known as "APT34" or "OilRig."

The attackers used a popular VPN service to disguise their location and make it appear as though the attack was coming from within the United States. They also used a custom-built malware tool that was especially designed to evade detection by security software.

At first, investigators believed that the attack was the work of a new threat group, due to the use of the VPN and the sophisticated nature of the attack. However, further investigation revealed that the attackers had made several mistakes that ultimately led to their identification, including leaving traces of their real IP address and using a tool that was linked to a previously known Iranian threat group.

The use of a VPN in this case allowed the attackers to create difficulties for investigators to attribute hacking activities, and may have been intended to mislead investigators or deflect blame onto a different group or country. However, the attackers ultimately failed to fully cover their tracks, and were eventually identified and attributed to a specific threat actor.

---

[14] For a review, see Al-Mulhim, R. A., Al-Zamil, L. A., & Al-Dossary, F. M. (2020). Cyber-attacks on Saudi Arabia environment. *International Journal of Computer Networks and Communications Security*, 8(3), 26–31.

[15] For an ethical overview, see Zhong, H., & Watters, P. A. (2020). The Ethics of Corporate Censorship of Information-Sharing Behavior: A Nonconsequentialist Perspective. *Library Trends*, 68(4), 697–711.

Summary

The examples described in this chapter show that disinformation and misinformation campaigns can have significant real-world consequences, especially in relation to the rules based international order. They pose a significant threat to democracies globally. Coordinated action is required to unmake and expose these operations and identify the perpetrators.

Chapter 11
Legal Issues in Cyber Counterintelligence

Transnational communication systems have created new challenges for counterintelligence efforts. Some of the main legal issues concerning counterintelligence in the cyber age include:

1. *Surveillance and privacy*: The use of surveillance tools to monitor potential threats in the digital space can raise concerns about privacy rights. Counterintelligence agencies must balance their need to gather information with the constitutional protections afforded to individuals.
2. *Hacking and cyberattacks*: Counterintelligence efforts may involve accessing protected computer systems or engaging in hacking activities. However, such activities can raise legal issues related to unauthorized access, data theft, and violation of intellectual property rights.
3. *International law*: Cyber activities can cross international borders, making it challenging to determine jurisdiction and legal frameworks. Counterintelligence agencies must navigate international law and diplomatic relations to effectively combat foreign threats.
4. *Human rights*: Counterintelligence activities must also adhere to human rights standards. Activities such as torture, detention without trial, or discriminatory practices violate human rights and can have legal consequences.
5. *Technology development*: The fast pace of technological advancements presents a challenge for counterintelligence agencies. They must ensure their activities comply with the law.

The risks to successful counterintelligence programs are not abstract. One legal challenge to counterintelligence in Europe has the balancing of individual rights to privacy against the need for intelligence gathering and national security. In particular, wiretapping, internet monitoring, and location tracking by intelligence agencies has been the subject of legal challenges in several European countries.

The European Convention on Human Rights (ECHR) promises the right to privacy, and the European Court of Human Rights has issued several rulings regarding

P. A. Watters, *Counterintelligence in a Cyber World*,
https://doi.org/10.1007/978-3-031-35287-4_11

surveillance technologies by intelligence agencies. For example, in the landmark case of Weber and Saravia v. Germany, it was held that the German government's use of a strategic telecommunications monitoring system violated the applicants' right to privacy according to human rights law in Europe.[1]

In response to such legal challenges, several European countries have established oversight mechanisms to ensure that intelligence agencies comply with the law and respect individual rights. In the UK, for instance, the Investigatory Powers Tribunal (IPT) is responsible for investigating complaints against intelligence agencies, and in France, the National Commission for the Control of Intelligence Techniques (CNCTR) oversees the use of surveillance technologies by a range of government bodies.

In the United Kingdom, the situation is even more complex. Brexit has the potential to affect the European Convention on Human Rights (ECHR) in a few ways:[2]

- *Withdrawal from the EU*: With Brexit, the UK has withdrawn from the EU which is separate from the Council of Europe, which oversees the ECHR. However, the EU has a charter of fundamental rights that is based on the ECHR, and Brexit could impact the future relationship between the UK and the EU with respect to human rights laws.
- *The Human Rights Act 1988*: This UK law that incorporates the ECHR into British law, allowing British citizens to bring legal actions within the UK. The UK government has indicated that it intends to change the Human Rights Act and incoprate a new Bill of Rights, although the details of this proposal are unclear at this time.
- *Potential Withdrawal from the ECHR*: There have been some calls from politicians and activists in the UK to withdraw from the ECHR entirely, citing concerns about judicial overreach and perceived limitations on national sovereignty. However, any such move would likely face significant opposition from both domestic and international stakeholders, and it is unclear at this time whether the UK government will pursue this course of action.

Whatever the political context, critics often argue that oversight mechanisms are insufficient, and that intelligence agencies continue to engage in surveillance activities that violate individual rights to privacy. This has led to ongoing legal challenges, particularly in cases involving emerging systems such as facial recognition and social media monitoring.

One noteworthy legal case involving facial recognition technology occurred in Illinois, United States, and is known as Rosenbach v. Six Flags Entertainment Corp.[3]

---

[1] For analysis, see O'Reilly, A. (2016). In defence of offence: Freedom of expression, offensive speech, and the Approach of the European court of human rights. *Trinity CL Rev.*, *19*, 234.

[2] A very complex situation! But for some bold predictions, see Charret-Del Bove, M. (2022). What Future for Human Rights in the UK Post-Brexit?. *Revue Française de Civilisation Britannique*, *27*, 2.

[3] For details, see Odden, M. (2022). Biometric Crisis: Legal Challenges to Biometric Identification Initiatives. *Wis. Int'l LJ*, *39*, 365.

The case involved a young boy who attended Six Flags Great America, an amusement park in Illinois, and had his thumbprint scanned at the park entrance as part of the park's biometric data collection system. The system used the thumbprint to create a unique numerical code that was associated with the plaintiff's season pass and used to verify his identity at subsequent visits to the park.

The plaintiff's mother filed a lawsuit against Six Flags, alleging that the park's use of biometric data without obtaining the plaintiff's written consent violated the Illinois Biometric Information Privacy Act (BIPA), a state law that covers personal biometric information, such as facial recognition data.

The plaintiff argued that his thumbprint was biometric data under BIPA, and that Six Flags had failed to obtain his written consent before collecting and storing it. Six Flags argued that the plaintiff did not suffer any harm because of the collection of his thumbprint, and therefore had no standing to sue.

The case eventually made its way to the Illinois Supreme Court, which favored the plaintiff. It was found that the thumbprint was indeed biometric data under BIPA, and that Six Flags had violated the law by collecting it without obtaining the plaintiff's written consent. The Six Flags' argument was rejected, ie, that the plaintiff had not suffered any harm, noting that the violation of a statutory right was sufficient to establish standing.

In summary, counterintelligence in the cyber age presents numerous legal challenges. Agencies must balance their need to protect national security with the rights and freedoms of individuals, all while navigating complex legal frameworks and technological developments.

Surveillance and the Law

Monitoring individuals and groups in any systematic way can raise a range of complex legal issues. Described below are some of the many relating to surveillance and the law that have arisen in recent times:

1. *Privacy*: Surveillance can interfere with an individual's right to privacy, which is often protected by laws or constitutional provisions. The legality of surveillance may depend on factors such as the location, the type of information being collected, and the way it is collected.
2. *Search and seizure*: In many cases, surveillance involves gathering evidence that may be used in criminal prosecutions. However, collecting evidence through surveillance methods may violate local laws and protections.
3. *Wiretapping or interception*: The use of wiretaps or interception devices to monitor electronic communications is subject to various legal restrictions, including obtaining a court order or warrant in many jurisdictions.
4. *Data protection*: Surveillance often involves collecting and processing large amounts of information, making compliance with data protection laws and individuals' rights a practical challenge.

5. *State secrets and national security*: In some cases, surveillance may be conducted by government agencies for national security purposes, such as combating terrorism or protecting state secrets. However, such activities must be consistent with constitutional and legal protections, including the need for transparency and accountability.

6. *International law*: Surveillance activities may also raise issues under international law, particularly when they involve the collection of information about foreign nationals or cross-border surveillance activities.

One noteworthy legal case involving wiretapping in Asia is the 2015 case of Najib Razak, the former Prime Minister of Malaysia, who was accused of wiretapping his political opponents and others.[4]

The allegations first surfaced in 2014, when a news website published transcripts of conversations between Najib and his associates, which appeared to suggest that he had been involved in the embezzlement of funds from a state-owned investment fund. Najib denied the allegations, and the government initiated an investigation into the leak of the transcripts.

However, the investigation soon widened to include allegations that Najib had ordered the wiretapping of his political opponents, journalists, and others who were critical of his administration. The government seized several computers and other equipment from the offices of a private investigation firm, which was believed to have been involved in the wiretapping.

Najib denied the wiretapping allegations, but several individuals associated with his administration were charged with offenses related to the wiretapping and the leak of the transcripts. The case sparked widespread protests and calls for Najib's resignation and was a major factor in his defeat in the 2018 general election.

In summary, surveillance is subject to a complex web of legal requirements and restrictions. The legality of surveillance will depend on various factors, including the location, data types, volumes, and purposes of the surveillance.

Search and Seizure of Data

Search and seizure on the internet in the US is a complex issue for law enforcement. Described below are some of the key laws and regulations relating to search and seizure on the internet:

1. *Constitutional Fourth Amendment*: Bans searches and seizures which are not reasonable, including those conducted on the internet. Law enforcement agencies generally require legal approval to conduct searches or seizures on the internet.

---

[4] For details, see https://www.malaysiakini.com/news/506387

2. *Electronic Communications Privacy Act (ECPA)*: Restricts access to stored electronic communications. It provides certain protections for the privacy of electronic data and a range of communications.
3. *Computer Fraud and Abuse Act (CFAA)*: The CFAA deals with hacking. It provides penalties for individuals who access computer systems without authorization, including those who engage in hacking activities.
4. *Digital Millennium Copyright Act (DMCA)*: The DMCA confers protections for intellectual property rights on the internet. It provides mechanisms for copyright owners to request the removal of infringing content from websites and online platforms.
5. *General Data Protection Regulation (GDPR)*: The EU GDPR governs the processing and protection of personal data. It provides certain rights to individuals over their data, such as the right to correct mistakes, and delete their data.

One noteworthy legal case involving the Digital Millennium Copyright Act (DMCA) is the 1999 case of Universal City Studios, Inc. v. Reimerdes.[5]

The plaintiffs in this case, which included several major Hollywood movie studios, brought a lawsuit against a group of defendants who had posted software code online that enabled users to bypass the copy protection mechanisms on DVDs. The plaintiffs argued that the software, known as DeCSS, violated the DMCA.

The defendants, including a college student named Jon Johansen, argued that DeCSS was a legitimate tool that enabled users to exercise their fair use rights to access and make copies of DVDs that they owned. They also argued that the DMCA's prohibition on circumvention was an unconstitutional restriction on free speech.

The courts ultimately held that DeCSS was a circumvention device under the DMCA, and that the defendants had violated the law by posting it online.

The Reimerdes case is significant because it was one of the first cases to test the DMCA's anti-circumvention provisions in court.

Many individuals have also been prosecuted under the CFAA since its enactment in 1986. One high-profile case involving the CFAA is the case of Aaron Swartz in 2011. Swartz had misused access to a vast digital library of academic journals through MIT. He was subsequently charged with wire fraud, computer fraud, and other offenses.[6]

Swartz argued that his actions were not illegal, and that he had accessed the articles as part of an effort to promote open access to academic information. However, he ultimately faced a very large potential sentence and financial penalties.

The case sparked widespread public debate about the CFAA and the broader issues of copyright law, freedom of information, and prosecutorial overreach. In

---

[5] For a recent analysis, see Asay, C. D. (2023). An Empirical Study of the DMCA's Anti-Circumvention Provisions. *Available at SSRN 4343160*.
[6] For analysis, see Thomas, A. J. (2023). Exceeding Authorized Access Under the CFAA. In *The Open World, Hackbacks and Global Justice* (pp. 211–261). Singapore: Springer Nature Singapore.

January 2013, Swartz committed suicide, prompting further scrutiny of the government's handling of the case.

Other individuals who have been prosecuted under the CFAA include Kevin Mitnick,[7] a notorious hacker who was charged with multiple violations of the CFAA in the 1990. Mitnick's hacking activities were primarily focused on gaining unauthorized access to computer networks and stealing sensitive information.

Mitnick's first major hacking incident allegedly occurred in the 1980s when he hacked into the computer system of a major corporation to steal software. He reportedly continued to engage in hacking activities throughout the 1990s, targeting a range of high-profile companies and organizations.

Some of Mitnick's reported and most noteworthy hacking exploits include:

*   *The hack of Digital Equipment Corporation*: In 1987, Mitnick allegedly hacked into the computer system of Digital Equipment Corporation and stole source code for the VMS operating system.
*   *The hack of Pacific Bell*: In 1992, Mitnick reportedly broke into Pacific Bell and took thousands of credit card numbers.
*   *The hack of Tsutomu Shimomura*: In 1995, Mitnick allegedly hacked into the computer system of security expert Tsutomu Shimomura and stole valuable research on computer security.

Mitnick was eventually arrested in 1995 and charged with multiple violations of the CFAA, went to jail after being convicted, and was released in 2000.[8]

Since his release from prison, Mitnick has become a cybersecurity consultant and public speaker, and has written several books about his experiences as a hacker.

In summary, search and seizure on the internet is a complex and multifaceted area fraught with danger for policing. Law enforcement agencies must balance the need to investigate and prevent crimes with the protection individual rights.

Safeguards and Abuses

There is potential for conflict between the Fourth Amendment and CFAA, particularly with respect to the issue of search and seizure of electronic information.

The CFAA criminalizes unauthorized access through hackong. It provides penalties for individuals who access computer systems without authorization, including those who engage in hacking activities. In some cases, law enforcement agencies may use the CFAA to obtain evidence of criminal activity without obtaining a warrant.

---

[7] For an overview, see Miftari, A., Luma-Osmani, S., & Idrizi, F. (2022, October). Analysis of cybercriminals and where they fall on the spectrum of crime. In *2022 International Conference on Data Analytics for Business and Industry (ICDABI)* (pp. 287–291). IEEE.

[8] For an account, see https://www.wired.com/2012/02/feb-15-1995-mitnick-arrested/

The use of the CFAA to obtain evidence of criminal activity without a warrant can raise Fourth Amendment concerns. In some cases, courts have found that the CFAA may be used to conduct searches and seizures of electronic information without a warrant, while in other cases, courts have required police to get a warrant prior to using the CFAA to conduct searches or seizures.

Law enforcement agencies must balance the need to investigate and prevent crimes with the protection of human rights and dignity, and must comply with applicable legal requirements and restrictions.

There have been several relevant cases that have dealt with the potential conflict between the Fourth Amendment and CFAA in the context of search and seizure of electronic information. Below are a few examples:

1. *United States v. Nosal (2012)*: In this case, the court found that the CFAA did not criminalize the misuse of computer information that was obtained with permission, and that overcriminalization was a legitimate and valid concern with the government's approach.
2. *United States v. Valle (2013)*: In this case, the court found that the prosecution via the CFAA of a police officer for accessing a law enforcement database for personal reasons without authorization violated the officer's Fourth Amendment rights.
3. *United States v. Warshak (2010)*: In this case, the court determined that the use of a warrantless seizure of emails violated the Fourth Amendment, and that people generally should have privacy in respect of their personal emails.

These cases highlight the potential for conflict between the Fourth Amendment and the CFAA in the context of electronic information and the need to balance law enforcement and privacy interests. The resolution of these conflicts relates always tp the specific facts and conditions of each lawsuit and may involve complex legal analysis and interpretation.

The Snowden case brought to light significant flaws in legal oversight of surveillance, particularly with respect to the collection and monitoring of electronic communications by government agencies such as the NSA.

Edward Snowden released classified documents in 2013 revealing the extent of the NSA's surveillance activities around the world such as phone call metadata. The disclosures sparked a global debate about privacy and government surveillance. Described below are some of the ways in which things have changed since Snowden:

- *Increased public awareness*: Snowden's disclosures brought the issue of government surveillance to the forefront of public consciousness, sparking a global debate about the balance between privacy and security.
- *Legal challenges to government surveillance*: Following Snowden's disclosures, there have been numerous legal challenges to government surveillance programs, both in the United States and abroad. Some of these challenges have resulted in significant rulings that have curtailed a range of counterespionage activities.
- *Increased use of encryption*: after the disclosures in this case, a significant increase in the use of encryption technologies by individuals and organizations

to protect their communications and data from government surveillance has been witnessed globally.

- *Changes in government policy*: In response to public pressure and legal challenges, some governments have made changes to their surveillance approaches. For example, the 2015 USA Freedom Act was passed in 2015, amended a number of controversial provisions of the USA PATRIOT Act.
- *Impact on international relations*: Snowden's disclosures have also had a significant impact on international relations, particularly between a number of allied countries. The disclosures revealed that the United States had been conducting surveillance on the communications of foreign leaders and diplomats, leading to a diplomatic fallout with some countries.

Legal Oversight of Surveillance Programs

Described below are some of the flaws in legal oversight of surveillance highlighted by the Snowden case:

1. *Lack of transparency*: The NSA's surveillance program was conducted in secret, and the public was not informed of its scope and scale until Snowden's disclosures. The government should always be accountable for its surveillance activities.
2. *Lack of judicial oversight*: The NSA's surveillance program was overseen by the FISC, a body that operates without the same level of transparency and accountability as traditional courts. The FISC approved almost all of the government's requests for surveillance, raising questions about the effectiveness of its oversight role.
3. *Basis of legal authority*: The government relied on a broad interpretation of relevant laws, particularly the Patriot Act, to justify its surveillance activities. Critics argued that the approach went beyond its intended scope and violated individuals' privacy rights.
4. *Lack of effective whistleblower protections*: Snowden's disclosures highlighted the lack of effective whistleblower protections in the United States. Snowden faced criminal charges and had to flee the country to avoid prosecution, leading some to argue that the government's response to his disclosures discouraged others from coming forward with information about government wrongdoing.

The Patriot Act has been controversial since its inception. Supporters argue that it has been effective in preventing terrorism, while critics argue that it has undermined civil liberties and privacy protections.[9]

---

[9] For a broad analysis, see Carter, J. (2022). *Counterterrorism Legislation: An Analysis of Three Federal Laws and Their Impact on US Counterterrorism Efforts* (Doctoral dissertation, Johns Hopkins University).

In terms of effectiveness, the evidence is mixed. Supporters of the Patriot Act point to several high-profile terrorism cases in which the law was used to gather intelligence and prevent attacks. For example, in 2009, the FBI used provisions of the Patriot Act to arrest Najibullah Zazi, planning to commit an act of terror. Similarly, in 2010, the FBI used the Patriot Act to arrest Faisal Shahzad, also caught engaged in terror.[10]

However, critics argue that the Patriot Act has not been effective in preventing terrorism and has instead been used to spy on innocent Americans. For example, much of the NSA's activities appear to have played no role in preventing terrorist attacks.[11] More challenging is that some provisions of the Patriot Act have been found to be unconstitutional.

In summary, the Snowden case and the outcomes of the Patriot Act highlighted the need for stronger legal oversight of surveillance ensuring that citizens are treated with dignity and respect for their personal data.

Transparency and Effectiveness

In addition to the lack of transparency and effectiveness in overseeing government surveillance programs, there have been several other criticisms made of the FISC.[12]

1. *Lack of Adversarial Process*: One major criticism of the FISC is the lack of an adversarial process, where the government can present its case for surveillance without any significant challenges from an opposing side. Unlike traditional courts where both sides present their arguments, the FISC only hears from the government and its lawyers.
2. *Rubber-Stamping*: Critics argue that the FISC has become a "rubber stamp" for government surveillance requests. From 1979 to 2012, the FISC approved more than 33,000 government surveillance requests and only denied 11. The perception that the FISC routinely approves these requests has raised concerns about whether it is an effective check on government power.
3. *Lack of Technical Expertise*: Another criticism of the FISC is that it lacks technical expertise to evaluate complex technical issues that arise in surveillance requests, such as the use of encryption or the interception of metadata. This can lead to the court relying too heavily on the government's interpretation of technical matters.

---

[10] For analysis, see SINAI, J. (2022). A Framework for Preempting Lone-Actor Terrorists During the Pre-Incident Phases. *Lone-Actor Terrorism: An Integrated Framework*, 304.

[11] For extensive analysis, see Carter, J. (2022). *Counterterrorism Legislation: An Analysis of Three Federal Laws and Their Impact on US Counterterrorism Efforts* (Doctoral dissertation, Johns Hopkins University).

[12] For a critique, see Kulshrestha, A., & Mayer, J. (2022). Estimating Incidental Collection in Foreign Intelligence Surveillance:{Large-Scale} Multiparty Private Set Intersection with Union and Sum. In *31st USENIX Security Symposium (USENIX Security 22)* (pp. 1705–1722).

4. *Limited Public Accountability*: The FISC operates in secrecy, and its decisions are not usually made public. How can the public to hold the court accountable for its decisions and to ensure that it is upholding the Constitution, if it is entirely secret?

These criticisms have led to calls for reform of the FISC, including proposals to increase transparency, introduce more adversarial procedures, and strengthen the court's technical expertise. The hope is that these reforms will lead to a stronger and more effective system for oversight of government surveillance programs.

There are several forms of civilian oversight of the US government's surveillance program, although the effectiveness and scope of these oversight mechanisms have been a subject of debate.

1. *Congressional Oversight*: Congress plays a critical role in overseeing government surveillance activities through various committees. These committees have the power to hold hearings, review classified information, and make recommendations for reform. However, critics argue that these committees have been ineffective in providing robust oversight, often being too deferential to the intelligence community.
2. *Executive Branch Oversight*: The Executive Branch also plays a role in overseeing government surveillance activities through various agencies. These agencies are responsible for providing legal guidance, reviewing surveillance requests, and ensuring compliance with laws and regulations. However, some critics argue that the Executive Branch has been too deferential to the intelligence community and has not done enough to rein in the surveillance program.
3. *Judicial Oversight*: As mentioned earlier, the FISC is responsible for overseeing government surveillance activities and is charged with evaluating whether surveillance requests are legal and comply with the Constitution. However, critics argue that the FISC has been too deferential to government requests and lacks effective transparency and accountability measures.
4. *Independent Oversight*: In addition to these oversight mechanisms, there are also independent bodies that provide oversight of government surveillance activities. For example, the Privacy and Civil Liberties Oversight Board (PCLOB) provides oversight and advice on privacy and civil liberties issues related to government surveillance activities. However, the PCLOB's authority and effectiveness have also been questioned by critics – PCLOB only has 11 staff members, including a chairman, four Board Members, and six professional staff members. This is somewhat modest compared to the NSA, with more than 30,000 staff.[13]

The United States has not been alone in reviewing legal protections in regard to counterintelligence in recent years. The European Union has implemented various measures to oversee and regulate counterintelligence activities across its member

---

[13] Shockingly, there is a suggestion by the Washington Post that the body has been dysfunctional for years, see https://www.washingtonpost.com/politics/2022/02/08/federal-privacy-watchdog-is-poised-come-back-dead/

states. These measures are designed to guarantee that counterintelligence activities are conducted in compliance with democratic governance.

One such measure is the EU's Common Foreign and Security Policy (CFSP), aiming to coordinate the foreign policy and defense activities of the member states. The CFSP contains provisions for intelligence sharing and cooperation among member states, as well as measures to combat terrorism and other security threats.[14]

The EU also has several institutions and agencies that are responsible for overseeing counterintelligence activities. For example, the European External Action Service (EEAS) implements the EU's foreign policy objectives through diplomatic means. The EEAS has a dedicated Intelligence and Situation Centre (INTCEN), which provides intelligence analysis and assessment to support EU policy. The EU INTCEN works closely with national intelligence services across the EU to collect and analyze information on security threats and other issues of concern.

Finally, the EU has also established various legal frameworks to regulate counterintelligence activities across member states. These frameworks include the EU Charter of Fundamental Rights, which outlines the fundamental rights and freedoms of EU citizens, and the GDPR which regulates the personal data utilization within the EU, as described above.

The legality of government surveillance in Asia varies from country to country. In general, most Asian countries have laws and regulations that govern the surveillance activities of their governments. However, the extent to which these laws protect privacy and limit the scope of government surveillance varies widely.

In some Asian countries, such as China, North Korea, and Vietnam, the government has significant control over the internet and telecommunications infrastructure, which allows them to monitor and censor online activity.[15] These governments often use national security laws to justify their surveillance activities, which can result in a lack of transparency and accountability.

In other countries, such as India and Malaysia, laws permit government surveillance but require strict adherence to procedural safeguards, such as obtaining a court order or warrant. However, there have been concerns raised about the implementation of these safeguards, and reports of abuse and overreach by government agencies.

Japan has also implemented a legal framework for government surveillance. The *Act on the Protection of Personal Information* regulates the collection, use, and storage of personal data by public and private entities, including government agencies. In addition, the Act on Wiretapping and Surveillance regulates the use of wiretapping and other surveillance techniques by law enforcement agencies.

Singapore and South Korea, as other examples, allow government surveillance under laws related to national security and public safety. However, there have been concerns raised about the lack of transparency and accountability in these countries' surveillance activities.

---

[14] For analysis, see Sjursen, H. (2003). Understanding the common foreign and security policy. *Understanding the European Union's external relations*, 29, 34.

[15] For a case study, see Watters, P. (2015). Censorship is ~~futile~~ possible but difficult: A study in algorithmic ethnography. *First Monday*.

In summary, while there are several forms of civilian oversight of the US and European government's surveillance programs, the effectiveness and scope of these mechanisms have been a subject of debate, with some arguing that they are insufficient to provide robust oversight of government surveillance activities.

International Law

International law deals with surveillance in several ways, including through treaties, agreements, and customary international law. Described below are some of the key international legal frameworks that address surveillance:

1. *International Human Rights Law*: generally provides a range of protections for the right to privacy. Governments are required to respect and protect this right, and any interference with it must be lawful, necessary, and proportionate.
2. *International Telecommunications Regulations*: The International Telecommunications Regulations, adopted by the International Telecommunication Union (ITU), aim to promote the development of the internet and other communications services, and ensure their efficient operation. They also address concerned about privacy and security, including the interception of communications.
3. *Cybercrime Convention*: The Council of Europe Convention on Cybercrime is the first international agreement that addresses cybercrime and includes provisions related to electronic surveillance. It requires signatories to criminalize certain types of cybercrime and to cooperate in the investigation and prosecution of such crimes.
4. *EU Data Protection Regulation*: The GDPR includes provisions related to the use of surveillance technologies, requiring that any surveillance be based on a legitimate legal basis and that individuals are informed of any surveillance that may affect them.
5. *UN Resolutions*: The United Nations has issued several resolutions that address surveillance and privacy.

In summary, international law aims to ensure that governments respect human rights and personal data privacy. It also seeks to promote cooperation among nations in the investigation and prosecution of cybercrime and to establish common standards for privacy and data protection.

How effective are these legal protections? It was revealed in 2013 that the NSA had been conducting surveillance on German Chancellor Angela Merkel and other high-level officials in Germany. The surveillance was carried out through the NSA's signals intelligence program, which involved intercepting phone calls and electronic communications.[16]

---

[16] For a German (!) perspective, see Weiler, M. (2014). The right to privacy in the digital age: The commitment to human rights online. *German YB Int'l L.*, *57*, 651.

The revelation of the surveillance activities caused a diplomatic rift between the US and Germany, with Chancellor Merkel expressing her displeasure and calling for an end to the surveillance. The incident also raised questions about the extent of US surveillance activities and their impact on diplomatic relations with other countries. In response to the controversy, President Obama ordered a review of US surveillance programs and proclaimed a series of reforms designed to increase transparency and oversight of intelligence activities.

The United States government is not subject to the GDPR or other European laws relating to surveillance. These laws apply to entities that operate within the European Union (EU) or European residents.

However, the US government is subject to the US Constitution and US laws, including those that regulate surveillance activities. In addition, the US government has entered into various international agreements and treaties that address privacy and data protection, including the Privacy Shield Framework. However, the Privacy Shield Framework was rejected by the European Court of Justice in 2020, and as of now, there is no agreement in place to govern cross-border data transfers between the EU and the US.

Please note that the US government has been criticized by European governments and privacy advocates for its surveillance practices, particularly those that involve the collection of personal data of non-US persons. The EU has raised concerns about the impact of US surveillance on the privacy rights of EU citizens and has called for increased transparency and oversight of US surveillance programs.

There have been several international conflicts that have arisen in relation to cross-border surveillance, particularly in cases where the surveillance has been carried out by one government on the citizens or residents of another country. Here are a few examples:

1. *The EU vs. the US*: As mentioned earlier, the EU and the US have had several disputes over US surveillance practices, particularly those that involve the collection of personal data of non-US persons. The EU has expressed concerns about the impact of US surveillance on the privacy rights of EU citizens and has called for increased transparency and oversight of US surveillance programs.
2. *China vs. the US*: The US and China have had several conflicts over cybersecurity and surveillance, with each accusing the other of engaging in cyber espionage and stealing intellectual property. The US has accused China of engaging in cyber-attacks against US companies and government agencies, while China has accused the US of using surveillance to spy on Chinese citizens and companies.
3. *Germany vs. Turkey*: In 2017, it was reported that the Turkish government had used a spy software developed by a German company to spy on Turkish citizens living in Germany. The German government expressed outrage at the use of the software and launched an investigation into the matter.
4. *Israel vs. Iran*: Israel and Iran have engaged in a covert cyber war, with each country accusing the other of using surveillance and hacking to carry out espionage and disrupt each other's infrastructure. In 2020, Iran accused Israel of car-

rying out a cyber-attack on its nuclear program, while Israel has accused Iran of using cyber-attacks to target Israeli infrastructure.

As an illustration of the legal complexity, Israel has not publicly disclosed the specific legal basis for its offensive cyber operations. Israel has stated that its use of offensive cyber capabilities is governed by international law. The IDF's Military Advocate General's Corps (MAG) has issued guidelines on the use of force in cyberspace, which state that Israel will only use cyber operations based on the principles of distinction, proportionality, and military necessity.[17]

The Israeli government has also passed several pieces of legislation related to cybersecurity, including the 2018 Cyber Defense Law and the 2002 National Cyber Bureau Law. These laws establish the legal framework for the security of critical infrastructure, the prevention of cyber-attacks, and the investigation and prosecution of cybercrimes.

It should be noted that while Israel has not publicly disclosed the legal basis for its offensive cyber operations, it is not uncommon for governments to keep such information classified for reasons of national security. However, Israel has been a vocal advocate of the need for international norms and regulations governing the use of offensive cyber capabilities. In 2019, Israel co-sponsored a United Nations resolution that called for the establishment of an operational entity to develop such norms and regulations.

In summary, cross-border surveillance and related cyber operations have become a contentious issue in the international community, with many countries expressing concerns about the impact of surveillance on individual privacy rights and national security. As a result, there have been calls for increased transparency and oversight of surveillance programs to ensure that they are conducted in a manner that respects human rights and international law.

Summary

Cross-border surveillance has led to several international conflicts, particularly in cases where one government conducts surveillance on the citizens or residents of another country. The conflicts have arisen over concerns about privacy rights and national security, and have involved countries such as the US, China, the EU, Germany, Turkey, Israel, and Iran. While there is no international law that specifically governs cross-border surveillance, there have been calls for increased transparency and oversight of surveillance programs to ensure that they respect human rights and international law.

---

[17] Whoever said hacking back wasn't legal! For justification, see Halberstam, M. (2013). Hacking back: reevaluating the legality of retaliatory cyberattacks. *Geo. Wash. Int'l L. Rev.*, *46*, 199.

Chapter 12
Ethical Issues in Cyber Counterintelligence

Counterintelligence in the cyber age raises several ethical issues, including:

1. *Privacy*: Counterintelligence activities in the cyber age often involve vast amounts of data being collected, raising issues concerning protection and safety of that data. The use of surveillance technologies such as monitoring software, facial recognition, and location tracking can violate the privacy rights of individuals and potentially undermine trust in democratic institutions.

2. *Accountability*: Counterintelligence activities in the cyber age can be carried out in secret, without proper oversight or accountability. This lack of transparency can lead to abuses of power in particular. There is also the risk that the information collected may be used for purposes beyond counterintelligence, such as political or economic gain.

3. *Bias and Discrimination*: There is a risk that counterintelligence activities may disproportionately target demographic groups using factors like gender, race, ethnicity, religion, or political beliefs. This can lead to discriminatory practices that undermine social justice and equality.

4. *Cybersecurity*: Counterintelligence activities can also have unintended consequences, such as compromising the integrity of computers and the internet. There is a risk that some tools and techniques used in counterintelligence may be exploited by hackers or other malicious actors, leading to data breaches and other security incidents. Think of Tor!

5. *International Relations*: The use of counterintelligence techniques in the cyber age can also raise tensions between countries and undermine international cooperation. The use of cyber-attacks or espionage can be seen as a violation of national sovereignty, leading to diplomatic incidents and potentially even armed conflict.

P. A. Watters, *Counterintelligence in a Cyber World*,
https://doi.org/10.1007/978-3-031-35287-4_12

One example of algorithmic bias in relation to national security is an algorithm to identify security risks among applicants for security clearances by the Department of Defense in the US.[1]

In 2019, the Defense Counterintelligence and Security Agency (DCSA), which is responsible for conducting background investigations and issuing security clearances for the DoD, introduced a new algorithm called the "Continuous Evaluation" system. The behavior of employees and contractors who hold security clearances is monitored, and flag potential security risks based on changes in their behavior.

However, a study by the Georgetown Center on Privacy and Technology found that the algorithm disproportionately flagged individuals from certain racial and ethnic groups as security risks, suggesting that the algorithm had inherent biases. The study found that the algorithm was twice as likely to flag individuals from certain minority groups, including African Americans and Latinos, as potential security risks, even when controlling for other factors such as criminal history.

This algorithmic bias raised concerns about the potential for discrimination and unfair treatment of individuals from certain minority groups. It also highlighted the need for greater transparency and accountability when using algorithms in similar contexts, and the importance of addressing potential biases and ensuring that algorithms are designed and implemented in a fair and impartial manner.

In summary, counterintelligence in the cyber age presents complex ethical challenges that require careful consideration of the potential impacts on privacy, accountability, bias and discrimination, cybersecurity, and international relations. Balancing these concerns will require ongoing dialogue and collaboration between governments, civil society, and the private sector to ensure that counterintelligence activities are undertaken based on sound ethical principles.

Cybersecurity

One consequence of the NSA mass surveillance program was that it potentially compromised the effectiveness of cybersecurity measures. The NSA's use of "backdoors" to access encryption keys and other sensitive information made it simpler for malicious actors to employ the same TTPs. In other words, the surveillance techniques that were meant to enhance national security may have made computer systems and networks more vulnerable to attack.

In the context of surveillance, backdoors are often used by government agencies to gain access to encrypted communications, such as emails or instant messages, without the knowledge or consent of the individuals involved. Backdoors can be installed on the computers or mobile devices used by the targets of surveillance, or

---

[1] For a broad discussion, see Golden, P. E. (2020). DoD's Artificial Intelligence Problem: Where to Begin. *Army Law.*, 76

they can be built into the software or hardware used to encrypt the communications.[2]

One example of a backdoor is a "key escrow" system, where encryption keys are held by a government agency, if they need to be accessed. Another example is the use of "vulnerabilities" – flaws in software or hardware that can be exploited to bypass security measures and gain access to sensitive data.

Backdoors are often controversial because they can be exploited by hackers or other malicious actors, who may use them to gain access to sensitive data or to control computer systems for nefarious purposes. There is also the risk that government agencies may abuse backdoors to conduct surveillance without proper oversight or accountability, potentially violating the privacy rights of individuals.

There have been instances where key escrow systems have been abused by governments in the past. One noteworthy example is the Clipper Chip, a key escrow system proposed by the US government in the 1990s. The Clipper Chip was designed to permit the government to obtain data from encrypted telecommunications by holding a copy of the encryption key, which could be accessed with a warrant.[3]

However, the Clipper Chip was widely criticized for its potential to undermine privacy and security. Critics argued that the system would simplify government access to conduct mass observation, and that it could be exploited by hackers or other malicious actors to gain access to sensitive data. In addition, the fact that the encryption key was held by a third party raised concerns about the potential for abuse or misuse by government agencies.

Ultimately, the Clipper Chip was never widely adopted, due in part to the controversy surrounding it. However, there have been other instances where key escrow systems have been realized, with mixed outcomes. The European Union, for example, has proposed a key escrow system as part of its efforts to combat terrorism, but this proposal has also been criticized for its potential to undermine security and privacy.

Furthermore, the NSA's actions damaged trust between the US government and technology companies, who were not informed about the program and who were pressured to cooperate with the agency's data collection efforts. This lack of trust made it more difficult for companies to work with the government on cybersecurity initiatives, reducing their effectiveness in combating cyber threats.

The revelation of the NSA's surveillance program also had broader international implications, with many countries expressing concern about the US government's disregard for privacy rights and the potential for abuse of power. This led to tensions between the US and other countries and may have hindered efforts to work together on cybersecurity and other global security issues.

---

[2] Very emotive topic! For details, see Lear, S. (2017). The fight over encryption: Reasons why congress must block the government from compelling technology companies to create backdoors into their devices. *Clev. St. L. Rev.*, *66*, 443

[3] For a retrospective analysis, see Blaze, M. (2011, December). Key escrow from a safe distance: looking back at the clipper chip. In *Proceedings of the 27th Annual Computer Security Applications Conference* (pp. 317–321).

In summary, the NSA's mass surveillance program is an example of how surveillance can undermine cybersecurity effectiveness by creating vulnerabilities and damaging trust between stakeholders. It highlights the importance of balancing the need for security with the protection of individual rights and the need for transparency and accountability in government surveillance programs.

Public opinion polls suggest that Americans have mixed views on the NSA's work, and this is no bad thing in a democracy. Some polls show that a majority of Americans support the agency's efforts to combat terrorism and protect national security, while others indicate that many Americans are concerned about the potential for the agency to overstep its bounds and violate privacy rights.

One major factor that has influenced public opinion about the NSA is the revelation of its surveillance activities by former contractor Edward Snowden, as outlined earlier. Since then, there have been ongoing debates regarding the appropriate mix of national security and personal privacy, and the role of the NSA in safeguarding both. Some Americans see the NSA as a necessary part of preventing attacks, while others view the agency as a potential threat to civil liberties and individual privacy.

In more recent years, the NSA has been credited with uncovering terrorist plots and disrupting terrorist organizations around the world. For example, the agency played a key role in identifying and tracking members of terrorist groups, and has helped to foil numerous other terrorist plots in the years since.

In summary, while opinions on the NSA vary among Americans, it is clear that the agency's actions have prompted ongoing debates about the appropriate balance between security and freedom in the digital age.[4]

Bias and Discrimination

There have been several cases where bias and discrimination have been identified in the use of surveillance and intelligence gathering by government agencies.

Recently, algorithmic bias has become a prominent concern as it is used by law enforcement agencies, and also more broadly by business for surveillance. Studies have shown that some facial recognition algorithms are less accurate when identifying individuals with darker skin tones or who are women, which can result in false positives and potentially discriminatory outcomes.[5]

There have also been concerns about potential bias in the use of social media monitoring by law enforcement agencies, which can disproportionately target marginalized communities and individuals. Critics argue that this can lead to the

---

[4] Not everyone is a cheerleader! For a review, see Etzioni, A. (2015). NSA: National security vs. individual rights. *Intelligence and National Security*, *30*(1), 100–136.

[5] It's a "thing" – for details, see Yucer, S., Tektas, F., Al Moubayed, N., & Breckon, T. P. (2022). Measuring hidden bias within face recognition via racial phenotypes. In *Proceedings of the IEEE/ CVF Winter Conference on Applications of Computer Vision* (pp. 995–1004).

stigmatization and persecution of innocent people, as well as violations of privacy and civil liberties.

A related issue is that of algorithmic bias, which arises when systems are designed or trained in a manner that results in unfair or discriminatory outcomes. This can occur when the algorithms are fed biased data or when they are trained on data that does not accurately reflect the full range of possible outcomes.

In the context of surveillance, algorithmic bias can result in inaccurate or discriminatory identification of individuals, groups, or behaviors. For example, facial recognition algorithms may be less accurate at identifying people with certain physical characteristics or from certain racial or ethnic groups, which can lead to false positive identifications or biased policing practices.

There have been several high-profile cases of algorithmic bias in surveillance and law enforcement, such as the misidentification of a suspect in a theft case in Detroit, where the technology misidentified the suspect as an innocent man with a similar appearance.[6]

These cases highlight the need for ongoing efforts to address algorithmic bias in surveillance and law enforcement, including the development of more accurate and fair algorithms, as well as increased transparency and oversight in their use.

The Right to Privacy

There are several ethical issues relating to privacy in counterintelligence, including:

1. *Invasion of privacy*: Counterintelligence activities, such as surveillance and information gathering, can involve intrusions into the privacy of individuals who may not be suspected of any wrongdoing. This raises questions about the balance between national security and individual privacy.
2. *Use of personal data*: Counterintelligence activities may involve biometrics or online activity, with no consent of the individuals involved. This can raise questions about the appropriate use and protection of personal data.
3. *Discrimination*: Counterintelligence activities may have the potential to lead to unfir treatment of groups based on their race, religion, or political beliefs. This raises questions about the fairness and impartiality of counterintelligence activities.
4. *Accountability*: Counterintelligence activities are often carried out in secret, which can make it difficult to hold those involved accountable for any abuses of power or violations of privacy. This raises questions about the need for transparency and oversight in counterintelligence activities.

---

[6] For details on the case, see Castelvecchi, D. (2020). Is facial recognition too biased to be let loose?. *Nature, 587*(7834), 347–350.

In summary, the ethical issues relating to privacy in counterintelligence involve balancing the desire for national security with legitimate concerns about human. It is important that counterintelligence activities are conducted in a way that is consistent with ethical principles and values, including transparency, accountability, and respect for individual privacy and human rights.

The US Supreme Court has recognized privacy as an important right, protected by the First, Fourth, Fifth, and Fourteenth Amendments, and the Constitution has been interpreted by the Supreme Court to include an expectation of privacy in certain areas, such as one's home, person, and effects. The First, Fifth, and Fourteenth Amendments have also been interpreted to protect privacy interests in various contexts, such as free speech and assembly, reproductive rights, and so on.

However, there is no right which is absolute, and safety, security and protection of broader social interests must also be considered. In cases where there is a conflict between privacy and other interests, the courts must balance these competing interests and determine the appropriate level of privacy protection under the circumstances.

There have been some relevant cases heard in recent years. Described below are some examples:

1. *United States v. Jones (2012)*: Examined the use of GPS tracking without a warrant. The court found that this activity actually required a warrant, leading to changes in the way that police approached similar cases in the future.
2. *Apple vs. FBI (2016)*: In the aftermath of mass killings in California, the FBI sought to compel Apple to divulge techniques to retrieve evidence from the shooter's iPhone. Apple did not comply, citing privacy concerns and the potential for the backdoor to be used by hackers or other governments. The case raised questions about the appropriate balance between privacy and law enforcement access to digital devices.
3. *Carpenter v. United States (2018)*: This case involved the collection of cellphone location data by law enforcement without a warrant. Similar to the first case above, the court also found that warrantless searches were inappropriate.

Apple's plan to monitor iCloud for Child Sexual Abuse Material (CSAM) has also raised questions about privacy and the potential for abuse. Under the plan, which was announced in August 2021, Apple would use a technique called "hashing" to detect known CSAM images stored in iCloud, and then report those images to law enforcement.[7]

While the goal of combating child exploitation is a laudable one, there are concerns that the monitoring could be used to violate user privacy or even be expanded beyond its original purpose. Critics argue that this monitoring could be the first step towards a more invasive surveillance regime, or that it could lead to false positives or errors that could harm innocent users.

---

[7] Needless to say, the very eminent Sarah Napier is a fan – for a review, see Teunissen, C., & Napier, S. (2022). Child sexual abuse material and end-to-end encryption on social media platforms: An overview. *Trends and issues in crime and criminal justice*, (653), 1–19.

Apple has responded to these concerns by emphasizing that the monitoring is only for known CSAM images, that it will be done in a way that preserves user privacy, and that it has put in place safeguards to prevent abuse. Nonetheless, the plan has sparked a debate about privacy and security, and the extent to which technology companies should be involved in monitoring their users.

International Relations

The release of classified information by WikiLeaks in 2010 was a significant event that raised concerns about privacy and national security.

WikiLeaks released a large amount of classified information from the US government, including diplomatic cables and classified military information about the post-9/11 wars. The release of this data was controversial and led to concerns about the impact on national security, diplomatic relations, and individual privacy.

Some argued that WikiLeaks' actions were a type of journalism and were safeguarded by fundamental rights and the public's right to know, while others argued that it put lives in danger, compromised national security, and violated privacy rights.

The release of this information also had significant political implications, leading to the resignation of several US government officials, and sparking international protests and debates about government transparency and accountability.

The publication of confidential diplomatic cables revealed frank assessments by US diplomats of foreign leaders and governments, including allies such as Germany, France, and the UK. This led to embarrassment, resentment, and mistrust among foreign officials and a perception that US diplomacy was manipulative and dishonest.[8]

For instance, the leaks showed that US diplomats had called the Italian Prime Minister Silvio Berlusconi "feckless, vain, and ineffective," and that the French President Nicolas Sarkozy was seen as an "emperor with no clothes." These revelations caused embarrassment and anger among these leaders and their governments and damaged the diplomatic relations between the US and these countries.

In addition, the leaks revealed the extent of US intelligence gathering operations around the world, including the surveillance of foreign leaders and diplomats. This created mistrust among allies and damaged the perception of the US as a trustworthy partner.

In summary, the WikiLeaks case highlights the complex ethical and legal issues related to privacy, free speech, national security, and government transparency. While there is a need for transparency and accountability in government, it is also important to balance this with the need to protect sensitive information and the privacy of individuals involved.

---

[8] Embarrassing for many, for a review, see McNair, B. (2012). WikiLeaks, journalism and the consequences of chaos. *Media International Australia*, *144*(1), 77–86.

The extent of US counterintelligence efforts is difficult to quantify as much of it is classified, but it is known to be a significant and wide-ranging endeavor. The US government has multiple agencies involved in counterintelligence, including the FBI, CIA, NSA, and DHS.

Counterintelligence efforts encompass a broad range of activities, including:

1. *Identification and prevention of foreign intelligence services* from obtaining sensitive information or compromising national security.
2. *Conducting investigations* and operations to counter espionage and sabotage.
3. *Protection of critical infrastructure*, trade secrets, intellectual property, and other assets.
4. *Counteracting foreign propaganda* and disinformation.
5. *Strengthening the security* of the government's own systems and networks.
6. *Providing training and education* to government employees and the private sector on counterintelligence best practices.
7. *Collaboration and cooperation* with international partners to address global threats.

The scope and scale of US counterintelligence efforts have increased in modern times, particularly in response to growing cyber threats and the increasing sophistication of foreign intelligence services. The US government has allocated significant resources to counterintelligence, including funding for research and development of advanced technologies, and hiring experts in cybersecurity and other areas of expertise.

Summary

Effective counterintelligence is always going to make adversaries unhappy, especially when threats or plots are uncovered by rigorous and robust investigations. However, good counterintelligence work must also keep an eye on broader relationships and the international goodwill on which cooperation depends, and remaining faithful to democratic norms and principles, and the international rules-based order.

Index

Printed in the United States
by Baker & Taylor Publisher Services

Printed in the United States
by Baker & Taylor Publisher Services